Caitlin

Better Homes and Gardens®

D0524721

Simple Soups
& Stews

Better Homes and Gardens® Books
Des Moines, Iowa

Our seal assures you that every recipe in *Simple Soups & Stews* has been tested in the Better Homes and Gardens® Test Kitchen. This means that each recipe is practical and reliable, and meets our high standards of taste appeal. We guarantee your satisfaction with this book for as long as you own it.

Copyright © 2003 by Meredith Corporation, Des Moines, Iowa.
First Edition.
All rights reserved.
Printed in China.
Library of Congress Control Number: 2003102428
ISBN: 0-696-21348-6

Pictured on front cover:
Hearty Turkey Soup, page 11

Better Homes and Gardens® Books
An imprint of Meredith® Books

Simple Soups & Stews
Editor: Carrie E. Holcomb
Contributing Editor: Mary Williams
Contributing Designer: Catherine Brett
Copy Chief: Terri Fredrickson
Copy and Production Editor: Victoria Forlini
Editorial Operations Manager: Karen Schirm
Managers, Book Production: Pam Kvitne, Marjorie J. Schenkelberg, Rick von Holdt
Contributing Copy Editor: Susan Fagan
Contributing Proofreaders: Gretchen Kauffman, Elise Marton, Donna Segal
Indexer: Martha Fifield
Electronic Production Coordinator: Paula Forest
Editorial and Design Assistants: Karen McFadden, Mary Lee Gavin
Test Kitchen Director: Lynn Blanchard
Test Kitchen Product Supervisor: Jill Moberly
Test Kitchen Home Economists: Judy Comstock; Marilyn Cornelius; Jennifer Kalinowski, R.D.; Maryellyn Krantz; Jill Lust; Dianna Nolin; Colleen Weeden; Lori Wilson; Charles Worthington

Meredith® Books
Editor in Chief: Linda Raglan Cunningham
Design Director: Matt Strelecki
Executive Editor, Foods and Crafts: Jennifer Dorland Darling

Publisher: James D. Blume
Executive Director, Marketing: Jeffrey Myers
Executive Director, New Business Development: Todd M. Davis
Executive Director, Sales: Ken Zagor
Director, Operations: George A. Susral
Director, Production: Douglas M. Johnston
Business Director: Jim Leonard

Vice President and General Manager: Douglas J. Guendel

Better Homes and Gardens® Magazine
Editor in Chief: Karol DeWulf Nickell
Deputy Editor, Food and Entertaining: Nancy Hopkins

Meredith Publishing Group
President, Publishing Group: Stephen M. Lacy
Vice President-Publishing Director: Bob Mate

Meredith Corporation
Chairman and Chief Executive Officer: William T. Kerr

Chairman of the Executive Committee: E. T. Meredith III

Contents

Welcome to Our Kitchen 4

Basics 5

Poultry 7

Meat 47

Seafood 87

Meatless 119

Sides 157

Index 187

Metric Information 192

Welcome to Our Kitchen

When you cook with a Better Homes and Gardens® cookbook, you can be confident that every recipe will taste great every time. That's because we perfect every recipe in our Test Kitchen before we present it to you.

Those of us in the Better Homes and Gardens® Test Kitchen have tested hundreds of recipes for soups and stews. And many recipes from years ago are still favorites with our readers and the Home Economists. A steaming bowl of beef stew or chicken noodle soup is as appealing to us today as it was to our grandparents.

Along with those time-honored dishes, soups and stews reflect current food trends and our passion for international and regional cuisines. Grocery stores are stocked with an ever-increasing variety of ingredients that bring new excitement to the stockpot. Other items such as frozen vegetables, precooked meats, and canned broths take much of the work out of soup making. We've combined the best of the old with the best of the new to create this collection of soul-satisfying recipes in *Better Homes and Gardens® Simple Soups & Stews.*

You'll find recipes to meet every taste and lifestyle demand. To help you sort through the recipes, we have flagged those that can be prepared in 30 minutes or less as **FAST**. If you're looking for low-fat recipes, check out the ones with this symbol: ♥. These recipes contain no more than 12 grams of fat per serving if a main dish or 5 grams if a side dish.

The Home Economists in the Better Homes and Gardens Test Kitchen are here to guide you through every step of every recipe. We've included some helpful tips that we use in the Test Kitchen as well as in our own homes. We hope this recipe collection will be a source of many pleasing meals for you and your family.

Lynn Blanchard

Lynn Blanchard
Better Homes and Gardens®
Test Kitchen Director

Basics

Before you reach for the soup kettle, take a few minutes to review these questions frequently posed to the Home Economists in the Better Homes and Gardens® Test Kitchen. Their answers ensure delectable results in every pot.

Q.

What do I use when a recipe calls for broth?

A.

You can make an instant broth using bouillon granules or cubes. For 1 cup, dissolve 1 teaspoon of granules or 1 cube in 1 cup of hot water. These products can be purchased in beef, chicken, fish, or vegetable flavors. Canned chicken and beef broths are even more convenient. Just be careful to check whether the broth is condensed. Condensed broths must be diluted with water before using. Other broths can be added to soup straight from the can. If you have the time, make your own broth using recipes in this book. Canned broths and broths made from bouillon tend to be saltier than homemade broths. Because the recipes in this book were tested with canned broths, you may need to add salt when using homemade broth.

Q.

When making broth or soup, how do I strain the liquid from the meat and vegetables?

A.

For the clearest broth, strain the mixture through 100-percent-cotton cheesecloth. Line a large colander with two layers of cheesecloth and place in a large heatproof bowl. Pour the broth mixture into the lined colander. Lift the colander and let the liquid drain through the cheesecloth. Discard vegetables and seasonings. When the bones are cool enough to handle, you can remove the meat and save it for another use. Discard the bones.

Q.

What is the best way to skim fat from broths or soups?

A.

To remove fat from hot soup or broth, use a large metal spoon and skim off the fat that rises to the top. If you're not serving the soup immediately, cover and refrigerate it for 6 to 8 hours or until the fat solidifies on the surface. Use a spoon to lift the solid fat from the soup.

Q.

Can I freeze leftover soups and stews?

A.

Many soups and stews can be frozen for up to 3 months. The best candidates for freezing are those containing meat or poultry and vegetables. Avoid freezing flour-thickened soups. The starch breaks down, altering the soup's consistency. Cheese soups also do not freeze well. Pasta and potatoes lose texture when frozen, so you may wish to avoid freezing soups with these ingredients as well.

Q.

How do I freeze and reheat soups and stews?

A.

Always cool foods before freezing. Transfer to freezer-safe containers. Use small, shallow containers to allow the food to freeze more quickly. Soups and stews expand when frozen, so leave ½ inch of space below the rim. Thaw frozen foods in the refrigerator or microwave—never at room temperature. You also can slowly reheat frozen food without thawing by placing it in an appropriate-size saucepan. Cook the food over low heat, covered, until it is thawed; stir occasionally to break it up. Then heat to boiling, stirring frequently. Before serving, be sure the solid pieces of food are heated through—not just the liquid portion.

Q.

How can I reduce sodium in soup and stew recipes?

A.

The most obvious way is to use homemade broths, which are generally much lower in sodium than commercial products. If you like, the convenience of canned, reduced-sodium chicken and beef broth is available. Also look for canned vegetables, beans, tomatoes, and tomato products labeled as reduced-sodium. If the vegetables or beans called for in the recipe are not available in reduced-sodium forms, substitute cooked fresh or frozen vegetables or cooked dried beans (see tip, page 28).

what's in a name?

A soup isn't always called a soup. Some soups go by other names.

- Bisque is a rich, thick, smooth soup that's often made with shellfish, such as lobster or shrimp.

- Chowder is a thick, chunky soup. Traditionally, a chowder is made with seafood or fish, but the definition has been expanded to include similar soups with poultry, vegetables, and cheeses.

- Stock or broth is a strained, thin, clear liquid in which meat, poultry, or fish has been simmered with vegetables and herbs. Vegetable stock is made with just vegetables. While normally used as an ingredient in other soups, broth also can be enjoyed as a light course on its own.

- Bouillon is basically the same as broth, but the term often refers to commercial dehydrated products sold as granules or cubes.

- Consommé is a strong, flavorful meat or fish broth that has been clarified (see tip, page 8).

Poultry

Catalan Chicken Chowder

In This Chapter:

African Chicken Stew 46
Asian Chicken Noodle Soup 15
Asian Turkey and Rice Soup 22
Brunswick Stew 41
Catalan Chicken Chowder 34
Chicken and Vegetable
    Bean Soup 13
Chicken and Wild Rice
    Soup 29
Chicken Broth 8
Chicken Chili with Rice 36
Chicken 'n' Dumpling Soup 10
Chicken Soup
    with Cavatappi 23
Chicken Stew with Tortellini 45
Chicken Tortilla Soup 27

Chicken Vegetable Ragout 44
Chili Blanco 38
Chipotle Chicken Soup 17
Classic Chicken-Sausage
    Gumbo 40
Creamy Broccoli-Chicken
    Soup 31
Creamy Chicken-Vegetable
    Soup 18
Easy Mulligatawny Soup 19
Easy Turkey Chowder 32
Fennel-Potato Soup 26
Garden Chicken Soup 9
Hearty Turkey Soup 11
Hot-and-Sour Turkey Soup 20
Indian Chicken Soup 12

Mexican Chicken Posole 21
Moroccan Chicken Stew 43
Pasta and Bean
    Chicken Soup 28
Quick-to-Fix Turkey and
    Rice Soup 24
Ranch Chicken Chowder 33
Southwestern Bean and
    Chicken Soup 25
Thai Chicken-Coconut Soup 16
Turkey and Sweet
    Potato Chowder 35
White Chili in a
    Bread Bowl 39

Chicken Broth ♥

Use this richly flavored broth in any recipe that calls for chicken broth or stock. If you make soup often, keep several cups on hand in your freezer (see tip, page 48).

Prep: 25 minutes **Cook:** 2½ hours **Makes:** about 6 cups

3 pounds bony chicken pieces (wings, backs, and/or necks)
3 stalks celery with leaves, cut up
2 carrots, cut up
1 large onion, unpeeled and cut up
1 teaspoon salt
1 teaspoon dried thyme, sage, or basil, crushed
½ teaspoon whole black peppercorns or ¼ teaspoon ground black pepper
4 sprigs fresh parsley
2 bay leaves
2 garlic cloves, unpeeled and halved
6 cups cold water

1 If using wings, cut each wing at joints into 3 pieces. Place chicken pieces in a 6-quart kettle or Dutch oven. Add celery, carrots, onion, salt, thyme, peppercorns, parsley, bay leaves, and garlic. Add water. Bring to boiling; reduce heat. Simmer, covered, for 2½ hours. Remove chicken pieces from broth.

2 Strain broth (see page 5). Discard vegetables and seasonings. If desired, clarify broth (see tip, below). If using the broth while hot, skim fat (see page 5). Or chill broth; lift off fat. If desired, when bones are cool enough to handle, remove meat; reserve meat for another use. Discard bones. Place broth and reserved meat in separate containers. Cover and chill for up to 3 days or freeze for up to 6 months.

Nutrition Facts per 1 cup: 30 cal., 2 g total fat (1 g sat. fat), 5 mg chol., 435 mg sodium, 1 g carbo., 0 g fiber, 2 g pro.
Daily Values: 1% calcium, 1% iron

clarifying stock

The secret to clear soups that sparkle and cream soups that are smooth is clarifying the stock or broth. To clarify stock, strain the stock and return strained stock to the Dutch oven or kettle. In a small bowl combine 1 egg white and ¼ cup cold water. Stir the mixture into the hot stock. Bring to boiling. Remove from heat and let stand 5 minutes. As the egg white cooks it will coagulate and trap fine particles from the stock. Line a large sieve or colander with several layers of damp 100-percent-cotton cheesecloth and place over a large bowl. Pour the stock through the cheesecloth to strain out the particles and egg white.

Garden Chicken Soup ♥

For a real treat, search out your local farmer's market for slender baby carrots. The packaged mini carrots commonly found in supermarkets are pieces of mature carrots and may take longer to cook.

Prep: 25 minutes **Cook:** 11 minutes **Makes:** 4 servings (about 9 cups)

1	tablespoon cooking oil
12	ounces packaged skinless, boneless chicken breast strips for stir-frying
3	cups reduced-sodium chicken broth
12	baby carrots (about 6 ounces with ½-inch tops)
2	medium onions, cut into thin wedges (1 cup)
2	cloves garlic, minced
1	large yellow summer squash, halved lengthwise and sliced (about 2 cups)
2	cups shredded Swiss chard
1	tablespoon snipped fresh lemon thyme or thyme
	Asiago cheese curls or Parmesan cheese curls*

1 In a very large skillet heat oil over medium-high heat. Cook chicken in hot oil about 3 minutes or until no longer pink.

2 Carefully add broth, carrots, onions, and garlic. Bring to boiling; reduce heat. Simmer, covered, for 5 minutes. Add squash and chard. Simmer, covered, about 3 minutes more or until vegetables are just tender. Stir in lemon thyme. Top each serving with Asiago cheese curls.

Nutrition Facts per serving: 217 cal., 8 g total fat (3 g sat. fat), 57 mg chol., 643 mg sodium, 12 g carbo., 3 g fiber, 26 g pro.
Daily Values: 231% vit. A, 25% vit. C, 11% calcium, 9% iron

*Note: Use a vegetable peeler to make thin curls of cheese from a wedge of Asiago or Parmesan cheese.

Chicken 'n' Dumpling Soup ♥ FAST

Greet the first days of autumn with a steaming meal-in-a-bowl topped with cheesy dumplings. For perfect dumplings, resist the urge to lift the lid and peek while they simmer.

Start to finish: 30 minutes **Makes:** 4 servings (about 6½ cups)

12 ounces packaged skinless, boneless chicken breast strips for stir-frying
⅛ teaspoon salt
⅛ teaspoon black pepper
1 tablespoon olive oil or cooking oil
2 tablespoons all-purpose flour
¼ teaspoon dried marjoram, crushed
1 14-ounce can chicken broth
1 cup water
1 medium onion, cut into wedges
1 cup fresh green beans, trimmed and halved, if desired
1 cup purchased julienne or coarsely shredded carrots
⅔ cup reduced-fat packaged biscuit mix
⅓ cup yellow cornmeal
¼ cup shredded cheddar cheese (1 ounce)
½ cup milk

1 Season chicken with salt and pepper. In a large saucepan cook and stir chicken in hot oil over medium-high heat about 2 minutes or until the chicken is no longer pink. Sprinkle flour and marjoram over the chicken. Stir in broth, water, onion, green beans, and carrots. Bring to boiling; reduce heat. Simmer, covered, for 5 minutes.

2 Meanwhile, for dumplings, in a medium mixing bowl stir together biscuit mix, cornmeal, and cheese. Stir in milk just until mixture is moistened. Drop batter on top of the bubbling soup, making 8 dumplings. Return to boiling; reduce heat. Simmer, covered, for 10 to 12 minutes or until a wooden toothpick inserted into a dumpling comes out clean. Do not lift cover while simmering. Transfer soup and dumplings to a deep serving bowl.

Nutrition Facts per serving: 345 cal., 11 g total fat (3 g sat. fat), 55 mg chol., 716 mg sodium, 35 g carbo., 3 g fiber, 25 g pro.
Daily Values: 87% vit. A, 8% vit. C, 13% calcium, 18% iron

Hearty Turkey Soup ♥

Fix this family-pleasing soup on a night you need to squeeze in a meal between activities. If dinner's late, you can keep the soup warm in your slow cooker. (Pictured on the cover.)

Prep: 25 minutes **Cook:** 6 hours **Makes:** 4 to 6 servings (about 6½ cups)

1   pound uncooked ground turkey
1   cup chopped celery
½   cup thinly sliced carrots
2½   cups tomato juice
1   14½-ounce can French-cut green beans, drained
1   cup fresh mushrooms, sliced ¼ inch thick
½   cup chopped tomato
1   tablespoon dried minced onion
1½   teaspoons Worcestershire sauce
1   teaspoon dried basil, crushed
1   teaspoon dried oregano, crushed
½   teaspoon garlic powder
½   teaspoon sugar
¼   teaspoon pepper
1   bay leaf

1 In a large skillet cook the turkey, celery, and carrots over medium-high heat until turkey is no longer pink and vegetables are tender; drain.

2 Place turkey mixture in a 3½- or 4-quart slow cooker. Stir in tomato juice, green beans, mushrooms, tomato, dried minced onion, Worcestershire sauce, basil, oregano, garlic powder, sugar, pepper, and bay leaf.

3 Cover and cook on low-heat setting for 6 hours. Remove and discard bay leaf before serving.

Nutrition Facts per serving: 245 cal., 10 g total fat (3 g sat. fat), 90 mg chol., 953 mg sodium, 17 g carbo., 4 g fiber, 23 g pro.
Daily Values: 106% vit. A, 80% vit. C, 9% calcium, 22% iron

keep a lid on it

When cooking foods in your slow cooker, resist the urge to lift the lid unless absolutely necessary. These appliances cook at such low temperatures that lost heat is not easily or quickly recovered. In fact, an uncovered cooker can lose up to 20 degrees of cooking heat in as little as two minutes. If you need to lift the cover to add ingredients, replace the lid as quickly as possible, especially when cooking on the low-heat setting.

Indian Chicken Soup ♥ FAST

Coriander, cumin, turmeric, and cilantro come together in this appealing, slightly exotic soup reminiscent of the vibrant cuisine of India.

Start to finish: 25 minutes **Makes:** 6 servings (about 8½ cups)

1 tablespoon butter

1 jalapeño pepper, seeded, if desired, and finely chopped (see tip, below) (optional)

1 teaspoon coriander seeds, crushed, or ½ teaspoon ground coriander

1 teaspoon cumin seeds, crushed, or ½ teaspoon ground cumin

6 cups chicken broth

2 tablespoons snipped fresh cilantro

½ teaspoon ground turmeric

1¼ cups dried small shell macaroni

2 cups sliced zucchini

1⅓ cups chopped tomato

2 cups chopped cooked chicken

1 In a large saucepan melt butter over medium heat. Add jalapeño pepper (if using), coriander, and cumin; cook for 1 minute. Add broth, cilantro, and turmeric. Bring to boiling; add pasta. Return to boiling; reduce heat. Boil gently, uncovered, for 6 to 8 minutes or until pasta is nearly tender.

2 Stir in zucchini and tomato. Return to boiling; reduce heat. Boil gently, uncovered, about 2 minutes more or just until pasta and zucchini are tender. Stir in chicken; heat through.

Nutrition Facts per serving: 244 cal., 8 g total fat (2 g sat. fat), 51 mg chol., 712 mg sodium, 23 g carbo., 1 g fiber, 21 g pro.
Daily Values: 7% vit. A, 18% vit. C, 2% calcium, 14% iron

handling chile peppers

Because chile peppers, such as jalapeños, contain volatile oils that can burn your skin and eyes, avoid direct contact with them as much as possible. When working with chile peppers, wear plastic or rubber gloves. In a pinch, work with plastic bags over your hands. If your bare hands touch a chile pepper, wash them thoroughly with soap and water.

Chicken and Vegetable Bean Soup

Fennel, tomatoes, and rosemary lend a Mediterranean note to this bean soup. Serve it with focaccia, a crisp green salad, and gelato for dessert.

Prep: 15 minutes **Stand:** 1 hour **Cook:** 8½ to 10½ hours **Makes:** 4 to 6 servings (about 11 cups)

1 cup dry Great Northern beans
6 cups cold water
1 large onion, chopped (1 cup)
1 medium fennel bulb, trimmed and cut into ½-inch pieces
2 medium carrots, chopped
2 cloves garlic, minced
2 tablespoons snipped fresh parsley
1 teaspoon dried rosemary, crushed
¼ teaspoon black pepper
4½ cups chicken broth
2½ cups shredded or chopped cooked chicken
1 14½-ounce can diced tomatoes, undrained

1 Rinse beans. In a large saucepan combine beans and the 6 cups cold water. Bring to boiling; reduce heat. Simmer, uncovered, for 10 minutes. Remove from heat. Cover and let stand for 1 hour. Drain and rinse beans.

2 Meanwhile, in a 3½- to 5-quart slow cooker combine onion, fennel, carrots, garlic, parsley, rosemary, and pepper. Place beans on top of the vegetables. Pour broth over all.

3 Cover and cook on low-heat setting for 8 to 10 hours or on high-heat setting for 4 to 5 hours.

4 If using low-heat setting, turn to high-heat setting. Stir in chicken and tomatoes. Cover and cook on high-heat setting for 30 minutes more or until heated through.

Nutrition Facts per serving: 426 cal., 10 g total fat (3 g sat. fat), 78 mg chol., 1,454 mg sodium, 46 g carbo., 15 g fiber, 40 g pro.
Daily Values: 176% vit. A, 42% vit. C, 16% calcium, 26% iron

Asian Chicken Noodle Soup FAST

Udon or soba noodles and miso (MEE-soh) give this soup Asian character. Miso is fermented soybean paste and a common flavoring in Japanese cuisine. Look for the noodles and miso in Asian markets.

Prep: 15 minutes **Cook:** 10 minutes **Makes:** 4 servings (about 6 cups)

2 14-ounce cans reduced-sodium chicken broth

1 cup water

3 ounces udon or soba noodles, broken in half (1 cup)

1 medium red sweet pepper, bias-sliced into bite-size strips (½ cup)

⅓ cup sliced green onions

1 tablespoon white miso

1 tablespoon grated fresh ginger

⅛ teaspoon crushed red pepper

1½ cups chopped cooked chicken or turkey

1 cup fresh snow pea pods, halved crosswise, or ½ of a 6-ounce package frozen snow pea pods, thawed and halved crosswise

Crushed red pepper (optional)

1 In a large saucepan combine broth and water. Bring to boiling. Add noodles. Return to boiling; reduce heat. Simmer, covered, for 6 minutes.

2 Stir sweet pepper, green onions, miso, ginger, and the ⅛ teaspoon crushed red pepper into broth mixture. Add chicken. Return to boiling; reduce heat. Simmer, covered, for 3 minutes. Stir in pea pods. Simmer, uncovered, for 1 minute more or until pea pods are crisp-tender. Ladle soup into bowls. If desired, sprinkle with additional crushed red pepper.

Nutrition Facts per serving: 225 cal., 6 g total fat (1 g sat. fat), 51 mg chol., 937 mg sodium, 22 g carbo., 2 g fiber, 23 g pro.
Daily Values: 16% vit. A, 75% vit. C, 2% calcium, 13% iron

Thai Chicken-Coconut Soup

Fish sauce adds a distinctive Thai taste. You can find this salty condiment in Asian markets or the specialty section of most supermarkets. Once opened, it will keep up to 3 months in the refrigerator.

Prep: 20 minutes **Cook:** 25 minutes **Makes:** 4 servings (about 9 cups)

1 pound skinless, boneless chicken breast halves or skinless, boneless chicken thighs
4 cups chicken broth
2 tablespoons fish sauce (optional)
2 tablespoons lemon or lime juice
1 tablespoon grated fresh ginger
1 teaspoon ground cumin
1½ cups broccoli florets
1 large red, yellow, or green sweet pepper, cut into thin strips (1 cup)
1 jalapeño pepper, seeded and chopped (see tip, page 12)
3 green onions, sliced into ½-inch pieces
2 tablespoons snipped fresh cilantro
1 14-ounce can unsweetened coconut milk

1 Cut chicken into bite-size strips. In a Dutch oven stir together chicken, broth, fish sauce (if desired), lemon juice, ginger, and cumin. Bring to boiling; reduce heat. Simmer, covered, for 10 minutes.

2 Stir in broccoli, sweet pepper, jalapeño pepper, green onions, and cilantro. Return to boiling; reduce heat. Simmer, covered, about 10 minutes more or until vegetables are tender. Add coconut milk; heat through but do not boil.

Nutrition Facts per serving: 461 cal., 33 g total fat (22 g sat. fat), 60 mg chol., 857 mg sodium, 9 g carbo., 2 g fiber, 31 g pro.
Daily Values: 10% vit. A, 99% vit. C, 23% iron

Chipotle Chicken Soup ♥

A half chicken breast graces each serving of this flavorful soup. If you like, bias-cut each breast half into ¼-inch slices and assemble them in the bottom of the bowl before ladling the soup on top.

Start to finish: 45 minutes **Makes:** 4 servings (about 6 cups)

3 14-ounce cans reduced-sodium chicken broth

1 canned chipotle pepper in adobo sauce, cut into 4 pieces

1 7- or 8-inch spinach, tomato, or plain flour tortilla, quartered

2 teaspoons olive oil

4 small skinless, boneless chicken breast halves (about 12 ounces total)

½ teaspoon ground cumin

2 teaspoons olive oil

1 small avocado, halved, pitted, peeled, and sliced

½ of a 14½-ounce can white or yellow hominy, drained and rinsed (about ¾ cup)

Dairy sour cream

Cilantro sprigs (optional)

1 In a 2-quart saucepan combine broth and chipotle pepper. Bring to boiling; reduce heat. Simmer, uncovered, for 20 minutes. Discard the pepper.

2 Meanwhile, for tortilla cones, place tortilla quarters on a clean white microwave-safe paper towel; microwave, uncovered, on 100% power (high) for 15 to 20 seconds or just until softened. Brush tortilla quarters with 2 teaspoons olive oil. Shape each into a cone; secure with a wooden toothpick. Place on a baking sheet.

3 Bake cones in a 375° oven for 8 minutes or until cones are light brown and slightly crisp. Cool slightly.

4 Rub both sides of chicken breasts with ground cumin. In a large skillet cook chicken breasts in 2 teaspoons hot olive oil over medium-high heat for 10 to 12 minutes or until chicken is tender and no longer pink, turning once.

5 To serve, place one cooked chicken breast half in each of four warmed soup bowls. Add avocado and hominy to each bowl. Pour simmering broth into each bowl. Spoon a small amount of sour cream into each tortilla cone. If desired, add cilantro sprig. Serve cones with soup.

Nutrition Facts per serving: 227 cal., 9 g total fat (2 g sat. fat), 52 mg chol., 895 mg sodium, 10 g carbo., 2 g fiber, 25 g pro.
Daily Values: 6% vit. A, 5% vit. C, 6% calcium, 10% iron

Creamy Chicken-Vegetable Soup FAST

A container of refrigerated Alfredo sauce replaces the white sauce that's the typical base of most cream soups. The sauce helps create a richly flavored soup that's ready in just 30 minutes.

Start to finish: 30 minutes **Makes:** 4 servings (about 8¼ cups)

3 cups chicken broth
2 medium carrots, thinly sliced
2 stalks celery, thinly sliced
1 cup chopped cooked chicken
1 small zucchini, thinly sliced (about 1 cup)
½ cup uncooked instant rice
1 10-ounce container refrigerated light Alfredo sauce
¼ cup chopped roasted red sweet peppers or one 4-ounce jar diced pimientos, drained
1 tablespoon snipped fresh thyme

1 In a Dutch oven combine broth, carrots, and celery. Bring to boiling; reduce heat. Simmer, covered, for 10 minutes.

2 Stir in chicken, zucchini, and rice. Remove from heat. Cover and let stand about 5 minutes or until rice is tender. Stir in Alfredo sauce, sweet peppers, and thyme; heat through.

Nutrition Facts per serving: 349 cal., 14 g total fat (7 g sat. fat), 65 mg chol., 1,286 mg sodium, 34 g carbo., 2 g fiber, 22 g pro.
Daily Values: 99% vit. A, 49% vit. C, 16% calcium, 12% iron

Easy Mulligatawny Soup ♥

This is an easy version of the golden-colored, curry-flavored soup from India. It's chock-full of apple, carrot, tomato, and chicken and spiced with curry and mace.

Prep: 20 minutes **Cook:** 20 minutes **Makes:** 4 servings (about 8 cups)

2 14-ounce cans chicken broth
1 14½-ounce can diced tomatoes, undrained
1 cup chopped apple
1 cup chopped carrot
½ cup chopped celery
⅓ cup long grain rice
¼ cup chopped onion
¼ cup golden raisins
1 tablespoon sugar
1 to 1½ teaspoons curry powder
¼ teaspoon coarsely ground black pepper
⅛ teaspoon ground mace or nutmeg
1½ cups chopped cooked chicken
1 tablespoon snipped fresh cilantro or parsley

1 In a large saucepan combine broth, undrained tomatoes, apple, carrot, celery, uncooked rice, onion, raisins, sugar, curry powder, pepper, and mace.

2 Bring broth mixture to boiling; reduce heat. Simmer, covered, about 20 minutes or until rice is tender. Stir in chicken; heat through. Stir in cilantro.

Nutrition Facts per serving: 297 cal., 5 g total fat (1 g sat. fat), 47 mg chol., 867 mg sodium, 39 g carbo., 4 g fiber, 22 g pro.
Daily Values: 156% vit. A, 33% vit. C, 9% calcium, 16% iron

Hot-and-Sour Turkey Soup ♥ FAST

This Chinese soup features the technique of cooking egg drops in flavored broth. The egg cooks in thin, swirling threads as you stir it slowly into the hot soup.

Start to finish: 30 minutes **Makes:** 4 servings (about 6⅔ cups)

3½ cups chicken broth
2 cups sliced fresh mushrooms
3 tablespoons rice vinegar or white vinegar
2 tablespoons soy sauce or reduced-sodium soy sauce
1 teaspoon sugar
1 teaspoon grated fresh ginger
¼ to ½ teaspoon black pepper
1 tablespoon cornstarch
1 tablespoon cold water
2 cups shredded cooked turkey
2 cups sliced bok choy
1 6-ounce package frozen pea pods
1 egg, beaten
3 tablespoons thinly sliced green onions

1 In a large saucepan combine broth, mushrooms, vinegar, soy sauce, sugar, ginger, and pepper. Bring to boiling.

2 Stir together cornstarch and cold water; stir into broth mixture. Cook and stir until thickened and bubbly. Cook and stir for 2 minutes more. Stir in turkey, bok choy, and pea pods.

3 Pour the egg into the soup in a steady stream while stirring 2 or 3 times to create shreds. Remove the saucepan from heat. Stir in green onions.

Nutrition Facts per serving: 238 cal., 6 g total fat (2 g sat. fat), 108 mg chol., 1,275 mg sodium, 15 g carbo., 4 g fiber, 30 g pro.
Daily Values: 4% vit. A, 49% vit. C, 7% calcium, 27% iron

Mexican Chicken Posole ♥ FAST

In parts of Mexico, posole is a traditional Christmastime dish. With this easy version you can make posole any day of the year as well as Christmas Eve.

Start to finish: 20 minutes **Makes:** 4 servings (about 6¾ cups)

12 ounces skinless, boneless chicken thighs or breast halves

3 to 4 teaspoons Mexican seasoning or chili powder

2 teaspoons cooking oil or olive oil

1 red or yellow sweet pepper, cut into bite-size pieces (¾ cup)

2 14-ounce cans reduced-sodium or regular chicken broth

1 15-ounce can hominy or black-eyed peas, rinsed and drained

Salsa (optional)

Dairy sour cream (optional)

Lime wedges (optional)

Shredded cheddar or Monterey Jack cheese (optional)

1 Cut chicken into 1-inch pieces. Sprinkle chicken with Mexican seasoning; toss to coat evenly. In a large saucepan cook and stir seasoned chicken in hot oil over medium-high heat for 3 minutes. Add sweet pepper; cook and stir about 1 minute more or until chicken is no longer pink.

2 Carefully add broth and hominy. Bring to boiling; reduce heat. Simmer, covered, about 3 minutes or until heated through. If desired, serve with salsa, sour cream, lime wedges, and cheese.

Nutrition Facts per serving: 192 cal., 8 g total fat (2 g sat. fat), 41 mg chol., 905 mg sodium, 14 g carbo., 1 g fiber, 15 g pro.
Daily Values: 21% vit. A, 52% vit. C, 2% calcium, 10% iron

Asian Turkey and Rice Soup ♥

If you know your morning will be hectic, cut up the turkey and vegetables the night before and refrigerate in separate plastic bags. In the morning, simply dump all the ingredients into the slow cooker.

Prep: 30 minutes   **Cook:** 8 to 10 hours   **Makes:** 6 servings (about 8½ cups)

2   cups sliced fresh mushrooms, such as shiitake or button
1½ cups sliced bok choy
1   medium onion, chopped (½ cup)
2   medium carrots, cut into bite-size strips (1 cup)
1   pound turkey breast tenderloins or skinless, boneless chicken breast halves, cut into 1-inch pieces
2   14-ounce cans reduced-sodium chicken broth
2   tablespoons reduced-sodium soy sauce
1   tablespoon toasted sesame oil (optional)
4   cloves garlic, minced
2   teaspoons grated fresh ginger
1   cup instant rice

1 In a 3½- or 4-quart slow cooker place mushrooms, bok choy, onion, and carrots. Add turkey. Combine broth, soy sauce, sesame oil (if desired), garlic, and ginger. Pour over vegetables and turkey.

2 Cover and cook on low-heat setting for 8 to 10 hours or on high-heat setting for 4 to 5 hours. Stir in rice. Cover and let stand for 5 to 10 minutes or until rice is tender.

Nutrition Facts per serving: 186 cal., 1 g total fat (0 g sat. fat), 47 mg chol., 584 mg sodium, 20 g carbo., 1 g fiber, 24 g pro.
Daily Values: 62% vit. A, 19% vit. C, 4% calcium, 11% iron

Note: Recipe may be doubled and cooked in a 5- or 6-quart slow cooker.

slow cookers

Some recipes in this book use a slow cooker, known as a "continuous slow cooker." Such cookers have heating coils that wrap around the sides of the cooker, allowing for continuous slow cooking. Note that intermittent cookers (those with heating elements or coils located below the food container) will not work for recipes in this book.

Chicken Soup with Cavatappi ♥ FAST

Cavatappi are corkscrew-shape noodles. Look for them near the macaroni in your grocery store. If you can't find cavatappi, use any short, thin pasta in this easy-to-make, amazingly flavorful soup.

Start to finish: 30 minutes **Makes:** 4 servings (about 8 cups)

- 2 carrots, bias-sliced into ½-inch pieces (1 cup)
- ⅓ cup finely chopped onion
- 2 cloves garlic, minced
- 1 tablespoon olive oil
- 4 ounces shiitake or button mushrooms, sliced (1½ cups)
- 4 14-ounce cans reduced-sodium chicken broth
- 4 ½-inch slices fresh ginger
- 1 bay leaf
- ⅛ teaspoon freshly ground black pepper
- 3 cups finely shredded kale or Swiss chard
- 2 cups chopped cooked chicken
- 1 cup dried cavatappi or elbow macaroni

1 In a large saucepan or 4-quart Dutch oven cook the carrots, onion, and garlic in hot oil over medium heat until onion is tender. Add the mushrooms and cook for 2 minutes more or until mushrooms are tender.

2 Stir broth, ginger, bay leaf, and pepper into vegetable mixture in saucepan. Bring to boiling. Stir in the kale, chicken, and pasta. Return to boiling; reduce heat. Simmer, covered, for 5 to 8 minutes or until the pasta and kale are tender. Discard ginger and bay leaf.

Nutrition Facts per serving: 342 cal., 10 g total fat (2 g sat. fat), 62 mg chol., 1,121 mg sodium, 33 g carbo., 3 g fiber, 32 g pro.
Daily Values: 244% vit. A, 107% vit. C, 10% calcium, 16% iron

Quick-to-Fix Turkey and Rice Soup ♥ Fa

Turn leftover Thanksgiving turkey into a meal your family will love with this simple soup. It's scrumptious when made with leftover roast chicken too.

Prep: 15 minutes **Cook:** 8 minutes **Makes:** 6 servings (about 8 cups)

4 cups chicken broth
1 cup water
¼ teaspoon dried Italian seasoning, crushed
¼ teaspoon black pepper
1 10-ounce package frozen mixed vegetables (2 cups)
1 cup instant rice
2 cups chopped cooked turkey or chicken
1 14½-ounce can diced tomatoes, undrained

1 In a large saucepan or Dutch oven combine broth, water, Italian seasoning, and pepper. Bring to boiling.

2 Stir in mixed vegetables and rice. Return to boiling; reduce heat. Simmer, covered, for 8 to 10 minutes or until vegetables are tender. Stir in turkey and undrained tomatoes; heat through.

Nutrition Facts per serving: 213 cal., 4 g total fat (1 g sat. fat), 35 mg chol., 687 mg sodium, 24 g carbo., 2 g fiber, 20 g pro.
Daily Values: 48% vit. A, 22% vit. C, 6% calcium, 15% iron

Southwestern Bean and Chicken Soup

Keep a package of frozen chopped cooked chicken, beans, and chile peppers on hand and you'll be able to prepare this peppy soup any day of the week.

Start to finish: 45 minutes **Makes:** 4 servings (about 7¼ cups)

1 large onion, chopped
   (1 cup)
1 tablespoon olive oil or
   cooking oil
2 14-ounce cans chicken
   broth
1 15-ounce can red kidney
   beans or Great
   Northern beans, rinsed
   and drained
2 4-ounce cans chopped
   green chile peppers
2 teaspoons dried oregano,
   crushed
1 teaspoon ground cumin
1 teaspoon garlic powder
⅛ teaspoon ground cloves
⅛ to ¼ teaspoon ground red
   pepper
3 cups chopped cooked
   chicken
  Shredded cheddar cheese
   (optional)
  Dairy sour cream
   (optional)

1 In a large saucepan cook onion in hot oil over medium heat for 3 to 5 minutes or until tender. Add broth, beans, undrained chile peppers, oregano, cumin, garlic powder, cloves, and ground red pepper. Bring to boiling; reduce heat. Simmer, covered, for 20 minutes.

2 Add chicken. Return to boiling; reduce heat. Simmer, covered, about 5 minutes more or until heated through. Ladle into soup bowls. If desired, serve with cheese and sour cream.

Nutrition Facts per serving: 377 cal., 13 g total fat (3 g sat. fat), 93 mg chol., 1,563 mg sodium, 26 g carbo., 8 g fiber, 43 g pro.
Daily Values: 10% vit. A, 68% vit. C, 8% calcium, 21% iron

the magic bean

Beans are hearty, filling, virtually fat-free, and a good source of fiber—especially soluble fiber. What's so important about fiber? For starters, soluble fiber can help lower blood cholesterol. Fiber also aids in digestion. Plus, a diet low in fat and high in fiber may help reduce the risk of some types of cancer. Beans also are high in protein, complex carbohydrates, and iron.

Fennel-Potato Soup

Light and dark rye croutons float atop bowls of this richly flavored, buttermilk-based soup. Make the croutons ahead of time and store them in a tightly covered container for up to one week.

Prep: 35 minutes **Bake:** 15 minutes **Cook:** 25 minutes **Makes:** 8 servings (about 12½ cups)

2 medium fennel bulbs (about 2 pounds)
6 medium potatoes, peeled and cubed (about 2 pounds)
4 cups reduced-sodium chicken broth
⅓ cup butter
½ cup all-purpose flour
½ teaspoon caraway seeds
½ teaspoon black pepper
2 cups cultured buttermilk or milk
2½ cups chopped cooked chicken
1 recipe Rye Croutons (optional)

1 Wash fennel. Snip ¼ cup of the leafy tops; set aside. If desired for garnish, set aside additional leafy tops. Cut off and discard upper stalks of fennel. Remove any wilted outer layers; cut off and discard a thin slice from the base of fennel. Halve, core, and chop remaining fennel. (You should have about 4 cups.)

2 In a 4-quart Dutch oven combine fennel, potatoes, and broth. Bring to boiling; reduce heat. Simmer, covered, for 15 to 20 minutes or until potatoes are tender. Drain, reserving broth. Set aside half the potatoes and fennel. Place remainder in a bowl; mash with a potato masher.

3 Meanwhile, in the same Dutch oven melt butter over medium heat. Stir in the flour, caraway seeds, and pepper. Add buttermilk. Cook and stir until slightly thickened and bubbly. Cook and stir for 1 minute more. Stir in the mashed potato mixture, the reserved chopped potatoes and fennel, reserved broth, reserved snipped fennel tops, and chicken. Cook and stir until heated through. If necessary, stir in additional broth to achieve desired consistency.

4 To serve, ladle soup into bowls. If desired, top each serving with Rye Croutons and reserved leafy fennel tops.

Nutrition Facts per serving: 334 cal., 13 g total fat (6 g sat. fat), 64 mg chol., 549 mg sodium, 36 g carbo., 16 g fiber, 20 g pro.
Daily Values: 10% vit. A, 26% vit. C, 10% calcium, 8% iron

Rye Croutons: Cut four ½-inch slices light and/or dark rye bread into ¾-inch squares; set aside. In a large skillet melt ¼ cup butter. Remove from heat. Stir in ¼ teaspoon garlic powder. Add bread cubes, stirring until coated. Spread cubes in a single layer in a shallow baking pan. Bake in a 300° oven for 10 minutes; stir. Bake about 5 minutes more or until cubes are dry and crisp. Cool. Makes 3 cups croutons.

Chicken Tortilla Soup

Fresh chile peppers guarantee that this ever-popular soup will boast a lively flavor. At the table, squeeze the lime wedges to add juice to the soup and further freshen the taste.

Prep: 20 minutes **Cook:** 15 minutes **Makes:** 4 servings (about 6 cups)

2   fresh Anaheim or poblano peppers, seeded and chopped (see tip, page 12)

1   medium onion, chopped (½ cup)

4   cloves garlic, minced

1   tablespoon cumin seeds

1   tablespoon cooking oil

2   14-ounce cans reduced-sodium chicken broth

1   14½-ounce can diced tomatoes, undrained

1   cup frozen whole kernel corn, thawed

1   cup coarsely shredded cooked chicken

¼   teaspoon salt

¼   cup snipped fresh cilantro

1½ cups coarsely crushed tortilla chips
     Shredded Monterey Jack cheese
     Lime wedges
     Diced avocado

1 In a 4-quart Dutch oven cook Anaheim peppers, onion, garlic, and cumin seeds in hot oil over medium heat about 5 minutes or until tender, stirring constantly. Add broth, undrained tomatoes, corn, chicken, and salt. Bring to boiling; stir in cilantro.

2 To serve, divide crushed tortilla chips among 4 bowls. Ladle soup into bowls over chips. Garnish each serving with cheese, lime wedge, and diced avocado.

Nutrition Facts per serving: 339 cal., 14 g total fat (3 g sat. fat), 31 mg chol., 1,015 mg sodium, 38 g carbo., 4 g fiber, 17 g pro.
Daily Values: 9% vit. A, 114% vit. C, 12% calcium, 17% iron

Pasta and Bean Chicken Soup FAST

Using canned beans, cooked chicken, and purchased pesto moves soup making into the express lane. Try this trattoria tip: Place a slice of grilled bread in each bowl and ladle the soup on top.

Start to finish: 25 minutes **Makes:** 5 servings (about 9 cups)

3½ cups reduced-sodium
    chicken broth
1 cup water
1 19-ounce can white kidney
    beans or Great
    Northern beans, rinsed
    and drained
2 cups chopped cooked
    chicken
1 14½-ounce can diced
    tomatoes with onion
    and garlic or diced
    tomatoes with basil,
    oregano, and garlic;
    undrained
1½ cups thinly sliced carrots
1 cup dried ditalini or tiny
    bow ties (4 ounces)
¼ cup pesto

1 In a large saucepan combine broth, water, beans, chicken, undrained tomatoes, carrots, and pasta.

2 Bring to boiling; reduce heat. Simmer, covered, about 10 minutes or until pasta is tender but firm. Stir in pesto.

Nutrition Facts per serving: 323 cal., 12 g total fat (1 g sat. fat), 46 mg chol., 914 mg sodium, 33 g carbo., 5 g fiber, 25 g pro.
Daily Values: 91% vit. A, 17% vit. C, 4% calcium, 15% iron

bean there, done that

Unlike canned beans, dry beans that you cook yourself are preservative-free and virtually sodium-free. When I have the time, I make a big batch and freeze in recipe-size amounts (thaw before using). To cook 1 pound of dry beans: Rinse beans. Bring beans and 8 cups cold water to a boil, reduce heat, and simmer for 2 minutes. Remove from heat. Cover and let stand for 1 hour. Or omit simmering and soak beans in cold water overnight in a covered pot. Drain and rinse. Fill the pot with beans and 8 cups fresh water. Bring to a boil; reduce heat and simmer, covered, until tender (at least 1 to 1½ hours).

Charles Worthington

Test Kitchen Home Economist

Chicken and Wild Rice Soup

Sliced leek, wild rice, and dry sherry combine to give this soup an elegant flair that's perfect for a casual dinner with friends. Pull a table up to the fireplace and ladle the soup into stoneware bowls.

Prep: 10 minutes **Cook:** 1 hour **Makes:** 4 servings (about 9 cups)

2   14-ounce cans chicken
       broth
1   cup sliced carrot
½   cup sliced celery
⅓   cup uncooked wild rice
⅓   cup sliced leek or green
       onion
½   teaspoon dried thyme,
       crushed
¼   teaspoon black pepper
2   tablespoons butter
3   tablespoons all-purpose
       flour
1   cup half-and-half or milk
1½ cups chopped cooked
       chicken
2   tablespoons dry sherry
     Thin carrot strips
       (optional)
     Snipped fresh thyme
       (optional)

1 In a large saucepan combine broth, carrot, celery, uncooked wild rice, leek, dried thyme, and pepper. Bring to boiling; reduce heat. Simmer, covered, about 50 minutes or until the rice is tender.

2 Meanwhile, melt butter; stir in flour. Stir in half-and-half. Cook and stir until thickened and bubbly. Cook and stir for 1 minute more. Slowly add half-and-half mixture to broth mixture, stirring constantly. Stir in chicken and sherry; heat through. If desired, garnish with carrot strips and fresh thyme.

Nutrition Facts per serving: 362 cal., 18 g total fat (10 g sat. fat), 85 mg chol., 785 mg sodium, 23 g carbo., 2 g fiber, 24 g pro.
Daily Values: 165% vit. A, 7% vit. C, 10% calcium, 11% iron

Pair a soup with a salad, a sandwich, or a basket of warm-from-the-oven bread and you have a complete meal. Here are a few ideas for items to serve with soups and stews.

Salad Combos

- Mixed greens, marinated artichoke hearts, halved cherry tomatoes, and strips of fresh mozzarella cheese with balsamic vinaigrette.
- Spinach, apple slices, and crumbled blue cheese with poppy seed dressing.
- Mixed greens, shredded carrot, sliced fresh mushrooms, and thinly sliced onion with creamy Italian dressing.
- Spinach, mandarin orange sections, and smoked almonds with citrus vinaigrette.
- Romaine lettuce, sliced fresh mushrooms, tomato wedges, and thinly sliced onion with Caesar dressing.
- Mixed greens, pear slices, and halved grapes with poppy seed dressing.

Sandwich Suggestions

- Jarlsberg cheese, prosciutto, salami, and thinly sliced honeydew melon on pumpernickel.
- Pastrami, provolone cheese, fresh basil leaves, and jarred roasted red sweet pepper strips on marble rye.
- Peppered turkey breast, romaine lettuce, and thinly sliced tomatoes stacked on a flour tortilla and rolled up.
- Cheddar cheese, ham, and thinly sliced apple on wheat bread. For a grilled version, spread both sides of the sandwich with butter and cook in a skillet over medium heat about 4 minutes per side or until cheese is melted.
- Smoked turkey breast, prosciutto, mixed salad greens, thinly sliced sweet onion, and provolone cheese in a hoagie bun. Drizzle with Italian salad dressing just before serving.

Easy-Fix Breads

Focaccia Breadsticks: Drain ½ cup oil-packed dried tomatoes, reserving the oil. Finely snip the tomatoes. Combine tomatoes, ¼ cup grated Romano cheese, 1½ teaspoons snipped fresh rosemary, ⅛ teaspoon black pepper, 2 teaspoons of the reserved oil, and 2 teaspoons water; set aside. Unroll one 10-ounce package refrigerated pizza dough. Roll dough on floured surface into 10×8-inch rectangle. Spread tomato mixture crosswise over half the dough. Fold plain half over filling; press lightly. Cut folded dough lengthwise into ten ½-inch strips. Fold each strip in half and twist two or three times. Place 1 inch apart on a lightly greased baking sheet. Bake in a 350° oven 12 to 15 minutes or until golden. Cool on a wire rack. Makes 10.

Green Onion Biscuits: Stir together one 5.2-ounce container boursin cheese with garlic and herbs and ¼ cup sliced green onions; set aside. Unwrap one 12-ounce package (10) refrigerated biscuits. Gently split the biscuits horizontally. Place the biscuit bottoms on a greased cookie sheet. Spread about 1 tablespoon of the cheese mixture over each biscuit bottom. Replace biscuit tops. Beat together 1 egg yolk and 1 tablespoon water. Brush biscuit tops with yolk mixture. Sprinkle with 2 tablespoons grated Parmesan cheese. Bake in a 400° oven for 8 to 10 minutes or until golden brown. Makes 10.

Creamy Broccoli-Chicken Soup FAST

This incredibly creamy soup is packed with vegetables, chicken, and just the right amount of seasoning. Ready in less than half an hour, it makes a family-pleasing supper for busy evenings.

Start to finish: 25 minutes **Makes:** 4 servings (about 6½ cups)

1½ cups small broccoli florets
1 cup sliced fresh mushrooms
½ cup shredded carrot
¼ cup chopped onion
¼ cup butter
¼ cup all-purpose flour
1½ teaspoons snipped fresh basil or ½ teaspoon dried basil, crushed
¼ teaspoon black pepper
3 cups milk
1 cup half-and-half or light cream
1 tablespoon white wine Worcestershire sauce
2 teaspoons instant chicken bouillon granules
1½ cups chopped cooked chicken or turkey
Coarse ground black pepper

1 In a large saucepan cook and stir broccoli, mushrooms, carrot, and onion in hot butter over medium heat for 6 to 8 minutes or until vegetables are tender.

2 Stir in flour, basil, and the ¼ teaspoon pepper. Add milk, half-and-half, Worcestershire sauce, and bouillon granules. Cook and stir until thickened and bubbly. Stir in chicken; heat through. Ladle soup into bowls and sprinkle with coarse ground pepper.

Nutrition Facts per serving: 435 cal., 27 g total fat (15 g sat. fat), 116 mg chol., 764 mg sodium, 23 g carbo., 2 g fiber, 26 g pro.
Daily Values: 109% vit. A, 51% vit. C, 33% calcium, 10% iron

Easy Turkey Chowder ♥ FAST

Opt for convenience when you select this off-the-shelf chowder. Count on the fresh basil and vegetables to round out the flavor.

Start to finish: 30 minutes **Makes:** 4 servings (about 5¾ cups)

1 cup small broccoli florets
1 medium carrot, coarsely shredded (½ cup)
½ cup diced peeled potato or ½ cup loose-pack frozen diced hash-brown potatoes
¼ cup chopped onion
2 cups milk
1½ cups chopped cooked turkey or chicken
1 10½-ounce can condensed cream of chicken soup
1 tablespoon snipped fresh basil
¼ teaspoon salt
¼ teaspoon black pepper
Fresh basil leaves, slivered (optional)

1 In a medium saucepan combine broccoli, carrot, potato, onion, and ½ cup water. Bring to boiling; reduce heat. Simmer, covered, about 6 minutes or until vegetables are tender. Do not drain.

2 Stir in milk, turkey, soup, snipped basil, salt, and pepper. Cook and stir over medium heat until heated through. Ladle soup into bowls. If desired, top each serving with slivered basil leaves.

Nutrition Facts per serving: 272 cal., 10 g total fat (4 g sat. fat), 59 mg chol., 825 mg sodium, 20 g carbo., 2 g fiber, 24 g pro.
Daily Values: 104% vit. A, 46% vit. C, 20% calcium, 10% iron

cooked chicken

When a recipe calls for cooked chicken and I don't have any, I purchase a deli-roasted chicken. A roasted chicken will yield 1½ to 2 cups boneless chopped meat.

Another option is to poach chicken breasts. In a large skillet place 12 ounces skinless, boneless chicken breast halves and 1½ cups water. Bring to boiling; reduce heat. Simmer, covered, for 12 to 14 minutes or until chicken is no longer pink (170°). Drain well. Cut up chicken as recipe directs. This will yield about 2 cups cubed cooked chicken.

Jill Moberly

Test Kitchen Home Economist

Ranch Chicken Chowder ♥

Sweet potato and serrano chile peppers combine to give this fast-to-fix chowder a sweet yet spicy taste. Bake a pan of corn bread to serve on the side.

Prep: 15 minutes **Cook:** 30 minutes **Makes:** 5 or 6 servings (about 8½ cups)

1 pound skinless, boneless chicken breast halves, cut into bite-size pieces
2 tablespoons butter
1 large sweet potato, peeled and sliced (about 8 ounces)
1 medium onion, chopped (½ cup)
1 to 2 fresh serrano chile peppers, seeded (see tip, page 12)
½ teaspoon ground coriander
¼ teaspoon ground cumin
3 cups chicken broth
1 14½-ounce can hominy, rinsed and drained, or 1 cup frozen whole kernel corn, thawed
   Snipped fresh cilantro (optional)
   Dairy sour cream (optional)

1 In a large saucepan or Dutch oven cook chicken, half at a time, in hot butter over medium heat until no longer pink. Remove chicken with a slotted spoon, reserving drippings in saucepan. Set chicken aside.

2 Add sweet potato, onion, serrano peppers, coriander, and cumin to saucepan; add half of the chicken broth. Bring to boiling; reduce heat. Simmer, covered, about 20 minutes or until vegetables are very tender. Cool slightly.

3 Place sweet potato mixture in a blender container. Cover and blend until smooth. Return mixture to saucepan; add chicken, remaining broth, and hominy. Heat through. Ladle soup into bowls. If desired, garnish with cilantro and sour cream.

Nutrition Facts per serving: 264 cal., 8 g total fat (4 g sat. fat), 66 mg chol., 689 mg sodium, 21 g carbo., 3 g fiber, 26 g pro.
Daily Values: 169% vit. A, 16% vit. C, 4% calcium, 9% iron

Catalan Chicken Chowder FAST

A package of saffron-flavored rice mix provides the Spanish seasonings in this chunky chowder. Artichoke hearts, roasted red sweet peppers, and toasted almonds further enhance the Spanish theme.

Prep: 10 minutes **Cook:** 20 minutes **Makes:** 4 servings (about 8 cups)

1 5-ounce package saffron-flavored yellow rice mix
8 ounces skinless, boneless chicken breast halves, cut into bite-size pieces
1 medium onion, chopped (½ cup)
1 clove garlic, minced
2 teaspoons olive oil
1 14½-ounce can diced tomatoes, undrained
1 14-ounce can reduced-sodium chicken broth
½ of a 14-ounce can artichoke hearts, drained and quartered (about ¾ cup)
½ cup loose-pack frozen baby sweet peas
½ of a 7-ounce jar roasted red sweet peppers, drained and cut into strips
2 tablespoons slivered almonds, toasted

1 Prepare rice mix according to package directions; set aside and keep warm.

2 Meanwhile, in a large saucepan cook chicken, onion, and garlic in hot olive oil over medium-high heat about 5 minutes or until chicken is no longer pink.

3 Add undrained tomatoes, broth, and artichoke hearts to chicken mixture. Bring to boiling; reduce heat. Simmer, uncovered, for 10 minutes, stirring occasionally. Add peas and peppers. Cook for 3 to 4 minutes more or until heated through.

4 To serve, ladle chowder into bowls. Spoon a mound of cooked rice into the center of each serving. Sprinkle with almonds.

Nutrition Facts per serving: 321 cal., 10 g total fat (2 g sat. fat), 30 mg chol., 1,099 mg sodium, 42 g carbo., 4 g fiber, 19 g pro.
Daily Values: 20% vit. A, 133% vit. C, 5% calcium, 23% iron

Turkey and Sweet Potato Chowder ♥

To get a head start on this soup, peel and cut up the potatoes, turkey, and parsley the day before. Refrigerate the potatoes, covered, in water, and the turkey and parsley separately in airtight containers.

Start to finish: 35 minutes **Makes:** 4 servings (about 8½ cups)

1 large potato, peeled and chopped (about 1½ cups)

1 14-ounce can chicken broth

2 small ears frozen corn on the cob, thawed

12 ounces cooked turkey breast, cut into ½-inch cubes (2¼ cups)

1½ cups milk

1 large sweet potato, peeled and cut into ¾-inch cubes (about 1½ cups)

¼ teaspoon black pepper

¼ cup coarsely snipped fresh Italian flat-leaf parsley

1 In a 3-quart saucepan combine chopped potato and broth. Bring to boiling; reduce heat. Simmer, uncovered, about 12 minutes or until potato is tender, stirring occasionally. Remove from heat. Using a potato masher, mash potato until mixture is thickened and smooth.

2 Cut the kernels from one of the ears of corn. Carefully cut the second ear of corn crosswise into ½-inch circles.

3 Stir corn, turkey, milk, sweet potato, and pepper into potato mixture in saucepan. Bring to boiling; reduce heat. Simmer, uncovered, for 12 to 15 minutes or until the sweet potato is tender. To serve, ladle chowder into bowls. Sprinkle with parsley.

Nutrition Facts per serving: 309 cal., 5 g total fat (2 g sat. fat), 66 mg chol., 381 mg sodium, 32 g carbo., 4 g fiber, 33 g pro.
Daily Values: 98% vit. A, 38% vit. C, 15% calcium, 13% iron

Chicken Chili with Rice ♥

Tomatillos, sometimes called Mexican green tomatoes, are often used in Mexican cooking. They hint of a lemon and apple flavor and impart their unique taste to this chunky chili.

Start to finish: 35 minutes **Makes:** 4 servings (about 5 cups)

3 cloves garlic, minced
1 fresh jalapeño chile pepper, seeded and finely chopped (see tip, page 12)
1 tablespoon cooking oil
2 cups frozen small whole onions
1 cup reduced-sodium chicken broth or regular chicken broth
2 teaspoons chili powder
1 teaspoon ground cumin
1 teaspoon dried oregano, crushed
1/4 teaspoon salt
1/8 teaspoon ground white pepper
1/8 teaspoon ground red pepper
1 19-ounce can white kidney (cannellini) beans, rinsed and drained
1 cup chopped cooked chicken
1 cup chopped tomatillos
2 cups hot cooked rice or couscous

1 In a large saucepan cook the garlic and jalapeño pepper in hot oil over medium heat for 30 seconds. Stir in onions, broth, chili powder, cumin, oregano, salt, white pepper, and red pepper.

2 Bring to boiling; reduce heat. Simmer, covered, for 20 minutes. Add beans, chicken, and tomatillos; cook and stir until heated through. Serve in bowls over rice.

Nutrition Facts per serving: 335 cal., 8 g total fat (1 g sat. fat), 34 mg chol., 417 mg sodium, 51 g carbo., 8 g fiber, 23 g pro.
Daily Values: 6% vit. A, 23% vit. C, 6% calcium, 26% iron

Chili Blanco ♥

You won't find tomatoes in this white chili, but you'll get plenty of heat from the fresh jalapeños. Gauge the hotness by the number of peppers you add.

Prep: 20 minutes **Cook:** 25 minutes **Makes:** 4 servings (about 7 cups)

12 ounces uncooked ground turkey

1 medium onion, chopped (½ cup)

1 12-ounce can or bottle beer or nonalcoholic beer

½ cup water

2 to 4 medium jalapeño peppers, seeded and finely chopped (see tip, page 12)

2 teaspoons instant chicken bouillon granules

1½ teaspoons chili powder

1 teaspoon ground cumin

2 15-ounce cans Great Northern beans or two 15- or 19-ounce cans white kidney (cannellini) beans, rinsed and drained

1 tablespoon lime juice

Dairy sour cream (optional)

Snipped fresh cilantro or parsley (optional)

Lime wedges (optional)

Chili powder (optional)

Bottled hot pepper sauce (optional)

1 In a large saucepan cook turkey and onion over medium-high heat until turkey is no longer pink and onion is tender; drain.

2 Stir in beer, water, jalapeño peppers, bouillon granules, chili powder, and cumin. Bring to boiling; reduce heat. Simmer, uncovered, for 20 minutes, stirring occasionally. Stir in the drained beans and lime juice. Cook 5 minutes more or until heated through.

3 If desired, mash half of the beans to thicken chili; stir. Ladle into bowls. If desired, garnish with sour cream, cilantro, and lime wedges and sprinkle with additional chili powder. If desired, pass pepper sauce.

Nutrition Facts per serving: 280 cal., 7 g total fat (2 g sat. fat), 32 mg chol., 818 mg sodium, 32 g carbo., 11 g fiber, 24 g pro.
Daily Values: 3% vit. A, 23% vit. C, 6% calcium, 27% iron

White Chili in a Bread Bowl ♥

For the bread bowls, look for individual loaves of sourdough bread at your local bakery. Or ladle the chili over fresh-baked corn bread squares.

Prep: 35 minutes **Stand:** 1 hour **Cook:** 1¾ hours **Makes:** 6 to 8 servings (about 9½ cups)

1 pound dry navy or Great
　　Northern beans
8 cups cold water
1 large onion, finely
　　chopped (1 cup)
2 cloves garlic, minced
2 tablespoons cooking oil
5 to 6 cups chicken broth
2 4½-ounce cans diced
　　green chile peppers
1½ teaspoons ground cumin
1 teaspoon dried oregano,
　　crushed
⅛ to ¼ teaspoon ground red
　　pepper
8 ounces skinless, boneless,
　　chicken breasts, finely
　　chopped
6 to 8 individual round
　　loaves of sourdough
　　bread or squares of corn
　　bread
　Dairy sour cream
　　(optional)
　Sliced jalapeño peppers
　　(see tip, page 12)
　　(optional)
　Shredded Monterey Jack
　　and/or Colby cheese
　　(optional)
　Salsa (optional)

1 Rinse beans. In a large Dutch oven combine beans and 8 cups cold water. Bring to boiling; reduce heat. Simmer, covered, for 2 minutes. Remove from heat. Cover and let stand for 1 hour. (Or omit simmering and soak the beans in cold water overnight in a covered pan.)

2 Drain and rinse beans. In the same Dutch oven cook onion and garlic in hot oil over medium heat until the onion is tender.

3 Stir in beans, broth, chile peppers, cumin, oregano, and ground red pepper. Bring to boiling; reduce heat. Simmer, covered, for 1½ to 2 hours or until beans are tender, stirring occasionally. Mash beans slightly to thicken.

4 Add chicken. Cover and simmer for 10 to 15 minutes more or until chicken is no longer pink. If desired, season with salt and additional red pepper.

5 Hollow out sourdough loaves or split squares of corn bread. Spoon chili into bread bowls or over corn bread. If desired, top with sour cream, jalapeño peppers, cheese, and/or salsa.

Nutrition Facts per serving: 632 cal., 8 g total fat (1 g sat. fat), 22 mg chol., 1,335 mg sodium, 100 g carbo., 19 g fiber, 40 g pro.
Daily Values: 1% vit. A, 26% vit. C, 18% calcium, 40% iron

Classic Chicken-Sausage Gumbo

Filé powder, made from ground sassafras leaves, is a traditional condiment to gumbo. Because it becomes stringy when boiled, add it just before serving the gumbo or pass at the table.

Prep: 15 minutes **Cook:** 40 minutes **Makes:** 4 servings (about 6 cups)

⅓ cup all-purpose flour

¼ cup cooking oil

1 medium onion, chopped (½ cup)

1 stalk celery, chopped (½ cup)

1 small green sweet pepper, chopped (½ cup)

4 cloves garlic, minced

¼ teaspoon ground black pepper

¼ teaspoon ground red pepper

2 14-ounce cans reduced-sodium chicken broth

1½ cups chopped cooked chicken or turkey

8 ounces andouille sausage or smoked sausage links, halved lengthwise and cut into ½-inch slices

1 cup sliced fresh okra or frozen cut okra

2 bay leaves

1 teaspoon filé powder

3 cups hot cooked rice

1 For roux, in a large heavy saucepan or 4-quart Dutch oven combine flour and oil until smooth. Cook over medium-high heat for 5 minutes, stirring constantly. Reduce heat to medium-low. Cook and stir about 15 minutes or until the roux is dark reddish brown.

2 Stir in onion, celery, green pepper, garlic, black pepper, and red pepper. Cook over medium heat for 3 to 5 minutes or just until vegetables are crisp-tender, stirring often.

3 Stir in broth, chicken, sausage, okra, and bay leaves. Bring to boiling; reduce heat. Simmer, covered, about 15 minutes or until okra is tender. Remove from heat. Discard bay leaves. Stir in filé powder. Serve in bowls with rice.

Nutrition Facts per serving: 680 cal., 36 g total fat (10 g sat. fat), 89 mg chol., 1,426 mg sodium, 50 g carbo., 4 g fiber, 37 g pro.
Daily Values: 8% vit. A, 44% vit. C, 8% calcium, 23% iron

Brunswick Stew ♥

Brunswick stew dates back to the days of colonial Virginia. Our updated version of the hearty dish features chicken and ham and simmers all day in your slow cooker.

Prep: 20 minutes   **Cook:** 8¾ to 10¾ hours   **Makes:** 6 servings (about 8½ cups)

3 medium onions, cut into thin wedges

2 pounds meaty chicken pieces (breast halves, thighs, and drumsticks), skinned

1½ cups diced cooked ham (8 ounces)

1 14½-ounce can diced tomatoes, undrained

1 14-ounce can chicken broth

4 cloves garlic, minced

1 tablespoon Worcestershire sauce

1 teaspoon dry mustard

1 teaspoon dried thyme, crushed

¼ teaspoon black pepper

¼ teaspoon bottled hot pepper sauce

1 10-ounce package frozen sliced okra (2 cups)

1 cup frozen baby lima beans

1 cup frozen whole kernel corn

1 In a 3½- or 4-quart slow cooker place onion. Top with chicken and ham. In a small bowl combine undrained tomatoes, broth, garlic, Worcestershire sauce, mustard, thyme, pepper, and hot pepper sauce; pour over chicken and ham.

2 Cover and cook on low-heat setting for 8 to 10 hours or on high-heat setting for 4 to 5 hours.

3 If desired, remove chicken; cool slightly. (Keep the lid on the slow cooker.) Remove meat from chicken bones; cut meat into bite-size pieces. Return chicken to slow cooker; discard the bones.

4 Add okra, lima beans, and corn to slow cooker. If using low-heat setting turn to high-heat setting. Cover and cook about 45 minutes or until vegetables are tender.

Nutrition Facts per serving: 322 cal., 9 g total fat (3 g sat. fat), 84 mg chol., 990 mg sodium, 24 g carbo., 4 g fiber, 9 g pro.
Daily Values: 7% vit. A, 33% vit. C, 11% calcium, 17% iron

Moroccan Chicken Stew ♥

A tantalizing blend of spices brings the exotic flavor of Morocco to this chicken and garbanzo bean stew. A handful of raisins sweetens the pot.

Start to finish: 35 minutes **Makes:** 6 servings (about 9¼ cups)

1 pound skinless, boneless chicken thighs
1 tablespoon all-purpose flour
1 teaspoon ground coriander
1 teaspoon ground cumin
1 teaspoon ground paprika
½ teaspoon salt
½ teaspoon ground cinnamon
2 medium onions, cut into wedges
3 cloves garlic, minced
1 tablespoon olive oil
1 28-ounce can crushed tomatoes, undrained
1 15-ounce can garbanzo beans (chickpeas), rinsed and drained
1½ cups water
½ cup raisins
⅓ cup small pitted ripe olives
3 cups hot cooked couscous
¼ cup snipped fresh cilantro

1 Cut chicken into 1-inch pieces. In a bowl combine flour, coriander, cumin, paprika, salt, and cinnamon. Add chicken to flour mixture; toss to coat. Set aside.

2 In a 4-quart Dutch oven cook onions and garlic in hot oil over medium-high heat about 5 minutes or until tender. Remove from Dutch oven, reserving oil in pan. Add chicken pieces, about half at a time, to pan. Cook and stir until lightly browned, stirring frequently.

3 Return all chicken and the onion mixture to pan. Add undrained tomatoes, beans, water, raisins, and olives. Bring to boiling; reduce heat. Simmer, covered, about 10 minutes or until chicken is tender, stirring occasionally. Spoon the couscous into 6 soup bowls. Ladle stew over the couscous and sprinkle with snipped cilantro.

Nutrition Facts per serving: 394 cal., 7 g total fat (1 g sat. fat), 60 mg chol., 858 mg sodium, 57 g carbo., 8 g fiber, 24 g pro.
Daily Values: 10% vit. A, 35% vit. C, 10% calcium, 19% iron

Chicken Vegetable Ragout

A ragout is a thick, rich French stew. Mop up this well-seasoned version with some crusty French bread and toss a crisp green salad to serve on the side.

Prep: 30 minutes **Cook:** 50 minutes **Makes:** 4 servings (about 4½ cups)

2 pounds meaty chicken pieces (breast halves, thighs, and drumsticks)
2 tablespoons cooking oil
1 large onion, chopped (1 cup)
8 ounces fresh mushrooms, quartered
2 cloves garlic, minced
1 tablespoon snipped fresh thyme or 1 teaspoon dried thyme, crushed
½ teaspoon black pepper
¼ teaspoon salt
1 bay leaf
2 cups chicken broth
½ cup dry white wine
4 medium carrots, cut into 1-inch chunks
4 parsnips, peeled and cut into 1-inch chunks
⅓ cup chicken broth
3 tablespoons all-purpose flour
Snipped fresh parsley (optional)

1 Skin chicken. In a 4-quart Dutch oven cook chicken in hot oil over medium heat for 10 to 15 minutes or until chicken is light brown, turning to brown evenly. Remove chicken; set aside.

2 Add the onion, mushrooms, garlic, thyme, pepper, salt, and bay leaf to Dutch oven; cook for 4 to 5 minutes or until vegetables are tender. Carefully stir in 2 cups broth and the wine. Add carrots and parsnips. Return chicken to Dutch oven. Bring to boiling; reduce heat. Simmer, covered, for 30 to 35 minutes or until chicken is tender and no longer pink and vegetables are tender. If desired, remove chicken with a slotted spoon and cool slightly. Remove meat from bones and cut into bite-size pieces; return chicken to vegetable mixture.

3 If necessary, skim fat from broth mixture. Discard bay leaf. In a screw-top jar combine ⅓ cup broth and flour; cover and shake until smooth. Add flour mixture to soup. Cook and stir over medium heat until thickened and bubbly. Cook and stir for 1 minute more. Serve in bowls. If desired, sprinkle with parsley.

Nutrition Facts per serving: 425 cal., 16 g total fat (3 g sat. fat), 92 mg chol., 714 mg sodium, 29 g carbo., 7 g fiber, 37 g pro.
Daily Values: 308% vit. A, 29% vit. C, 8% calcium, 18% iron

Chicken Stew with Tortellini ♥

Dress up leftover chicken by stirring it into this easy stew. Chunks of yellow squash and sweet pepper accompany plump tortellini and beet greens.

Start to finish: 35 minutes **Makes:** 6 servings (about 7½ cups)

2 cups water

1 14-ounce can reduced-sodium chicken broth

1 medium yellow summer squash

6 cups torn beet greens, turnip greens, or spinach

1 green sweet pepper, coarsely chopped

1 cup dried cheese-filled tortellini pasta

1 medium onion, cut into thin wedges

1 medium carrot, sliced

1½ teaspoons snipped fresh rosemary

½ teaspoon salt-free seasoning blend

¼ teaspoon black pepper

2 cups chopped cooked chicken

1 tablespoon snipped fresh basil

1 In a Dutch oven bring water and broth to boiling. Meanwhile, halve summer squash lengthwise and cut into ½-inch slices. Add squash, greens, sweet pepper, pasta, onion, carrot, rosemary, seasoning blend, and black pepper to Dutch oven.

2 Return to boiling; reduce heat. Simmer, covered, about 15 minutes or until pasta and vegetables are nearly tender.

3 Stir in chicken. Return to boiling; reduce heat. Simmer, covered, about 5 minutes more or until pasta and vegetables are tender. Stir fresh basil into soup.

Nutrition Facts per serving: 234 cal., 6 g total fat (1 g sat. fat), 45 mg chol., 530 mg sodium, 22 g carbo., 3 g fiber, 22 g pro.
Daily Values: 114% vit. A, 55% vit. C, 14% calcium, 13% iron

African Chicken Stew

Peanut butter lends pleasing body as well as flavor to this thick stew. Dried chile peppers and fresh ginger add extra punch.

Prep: 30 minutes **Cook:** 50 minutes **Makes:** 8 servings (about 10 cups)

2	2½- to 3-pound broiler-fryer chickens, cut up
6	cups water
1	medium onion, halved
4	teaspoons grated fresh ginger or 2 teaspoons ground ginger
2	large onions, chopped (2 cups)
2	tablespoons peanut oil
¼	cup tomato paste
2	large tomatoes, chopped (2 cups)
1	cup peanut butter
4	small dried hot chile peppers, crushed, or 2 teaspoons crushed red pepper
½	teaspoon salt
4	cups hot cooked rice
½	cup chopped peanuts

1 If desired, skin chickens. In a 6- to 8-quart Dutch oven combine chicken, water, halved onion, and ginger. Bring to boiling; reduce heat. Simmer, covered, about 35 minutes or until chicken is tender and no longer pink.

2 Remove chicken. Strain broth (see page 5); discard onion. Skim fat from broth (see page 5); set broth aside. When chicken is cool enough to handle, remove meat from bones; discard skin (if present) and bones. Chop meat; set aside.

3 Meanwhile, in a 4-quart Dutch oven cook chopped onion in hot oil over medium heat for 5 minutes. Stir in tomato paste. Add the chicken, tomatoes, and 3 cups of the broth. Stir in peanut butter, chile peppers, and salt. If necessary, stir in additional broth to achieve the consistency of a thick stew. Bring to boiling; reduce heat. Simmer, uncovered, for 15 minutes, stirring occasionally. Add broth as needed to maintain desired consistency (reserve remaining broth for another use).

4 To serve, spoon rice into soup bowls. Add stew; sprinkle with chopped peanuts.

Nutrition Facts per serving: 572 cal., 29 g total fat (6 g sat. fat), 95 mg chol., 456 mg sodium, 38 g carbo., 5 g fiber, 43 g pro.
Daily Values: 8% vit. A, 27% vit. C, 6% calcium, 19% iron

Meat

Ham and Vegetable Soup

In This Chapter:

Beef and Red Bean Chili 58
Beef Broth 48
Beef Ragout 86
Beef Stew with Lentils 64
Beefy Vegetable Soup 49
Bratwurst and Potato Soup 71
Carbonnade of Beef
    and Vegetables 65
Cassoulet-Style Stew 84
Chili with Cornmeal
    Dumplings 57
Chinese Beef and
    Noodle Soup 51
Chunky Ham and
    Potato Chowder 75

Corny Sausage Chowder 77
Creamy Ham and
    Vegetable Stew 78
Curried Pumpkin Soup 67
Curried Split Pea Soup 72
Endive, Ham, and
    Bean Soup 70
Gingersnap Stew 79
Green Chile Stew 62
Ham and Vegetable Soup 68
Hamburger Soup 54
Hearty Rice and
    Sausage Soup 66
Italian Beef Soup 55
Italian Chili 60
Italian Wedding Soup 52

Lamb, Lentil, and
    Onion Soup 81
Lamb Stew with Couscous 85
Lamb Stew with
    Sweet Potatoes 83
Lentil and Sausage Soup 73
Meatball Soup 50
New England Ham and
    Pea Soup 69
Old-Time Beef Stew 63
Pork and Mushroom Soup 74
Pork and Orzo Soup
    with Spinach 80
Salsa Verde Beef Stew 61
Tex-Mex Chili 56

Beef Broth ♥

Depending on the meatiness of your soup bones, they'll yield 3 to 4 cups of meat. Use this cooked meat in soups, stews, and casseroles.

Prep: 30 minutes **Bake:** 30 minutes **Cook:** 3½ hours **Makes:** 8 to 9 cups

4	pounds meaty beef soup bones (beef shank cross cuts or short ribs)
½	cup water
3	carrots, cut up
2	medium onions, unpeeled and cut up
2	stalks celery with leaves, cut up
1	tablespoon dried basil or thyme, crushed
1½	teaspoons salt
10	whole black peppercorns
8	sprigs fresh parsley
4	bay leaves
2	cloves garlic, unpeeled and halved
10	cups water

1 Place soup bones in a large shallow roasting pan. Bake in a 450° oven about 30 minutes or until well browned, turning once. Place soup bones in a large kettle or Dutch oven. Pour the ½ cup water into the roasting pan, scraping up browned bits; add water mixture to kettle. Stir in carrots, onions, celery, basil, salt, peppercorns, parsley, bay leaves, and garlic. Add the 10 cups water. Bring to boiling; reduce heat. Simmer, covered, for 3½ hours. Remove soup bones.

2 Strain broth (see page 5). Discard vegetables and seasonings. If desired, clarify broth (see tip, page 8). If using the broth while hot, skim fat (see page 5). Or chill broth; lift off fat. If desired, when bones are cool enough to handle, remove meat; reserve meat for another use. Discard bones. Place broth and reserved meat in separate containers. Cover and chill for up to 3 days or freeze for up to 6 months.

Nutrition Facts per 1 cup: 20 cal., 1 g total fat (5 g sat. fat), 1 mg chol., 409 mg sodium, 2 g carbo., 0 g fiber, 2 g pro.
Daily Values: 1% calcium, 1% iron

freezing broth and stock

I like to keep a supply of homemade broth in the freezer. To freeze broth, pour the cooled broth into 1- or 2-cup airtight containers, leaving about ½ inch of headspace at the top to allow for the broth to expand. Seal, label, and freeze for up to 6 months. Thaw the broth overnight in the refrigerator. To quick-thaw the broth, heat it in the microwave oven or in a saucepan on top of the stove. You also can store broth, tightly covered, for up to 3 days in your refrigerator.

Colleen Weeden
Test Kitchen Home Economist

Beefy Vegetable Soup

For easy retrieval, the herbs, celery leaves, and garlic are placed in cheesecloth bundles. Be sure to use cheesecloth made from 100-percent cotton.

Prep: 20 minutes **Cook:** 2¼ hours **Makes:** 6 servings (about 8 cups)

2½ pounds beef shank
    cross cuts
3 cups water
2 teaspoons instant beef
    bouillon granules
1 teaspoon salt
½ teaspoon black pepper
4 sprigs fresh parsley
    Celery leaves from 3 stalks
2 bay leaves
2 cloves garlic, halved
4 sprigs fresh thyme
2 cups chopped, peeled
    tomatoes
1½ cups peeled sweet
    potatoes cut into ¾-inch
    cubes
1 cup sliced parsnips
1 cup sliced carrot
1 cup sliced celery
2 cups fresh pea pods,
    halved crosswise

1 Trim fat from beef shanks. In a large Dutch oven combine meat, water, bouillon granules, salt, and pepper. Place parsley, celery leaves, bay leaves, garlic, and thyme on a 10-inch-square double thickness of 100-percent-cotton cheesecloth. Tie cheesecloth into a bag with a clean string; add to Dutch oven. Bring to boiling; reduce heat. Simmer, covered, for 2 hours. Remove from heat.

2 Remove meat from soup; set aside to cool slightly. When cool enough to handle, cut meat off bones and coarsely chop; discard bones. Skim fat from broth (see page 5). Add meat, tomatoes, sweet potatoes, parsnips, carrot, and celery to broth.

3 Return meat mixture to boiling; reduce heat. Simmer, covered, for 15 minutes. Stir in pea pods; simmer, covered, for 1 to 2 minutes more or until the pea pods are crisp-tender. Discard cheesecloth bag. Season to taste with salt and pepper.

Nutrition Facts per serving: 235 cal., 5 g total fat (2 g sat. fat), 55 mg chol., 758 mg sodium, 21 g carbo., 5 g fiber, 27 g pro.
Daily Values: 232% vit. A, 66% vit. C, 7% calcium, 21% iron

To Make Ahead: Prepare soup as directed, except do not add pea pods. Pour soup into a storage container. Cover and chill for up to 24 hours. To serve, transfer mixture to Dutch oven. Cook over medium-low heat until heated through. Add pea pods; simmer, covered, for 1 to 2 minutes or until pea pods are crisp-tender.

Meatball Soup

This full-flavored Italian-style soup features pasta, garbanzo beans, spinach, and spoon-size meatballs. Sprinkle individual servings with finely shredded Parmesan cheese, if you like.

Prep: 35 minutes **Cook:** 12 minutes **Makes:** 4 servings (about 7 cups)

1 beaten egg
½ cup soft bread crumbs (⅔ slice)
2 tablespoons finely shredded Parmesan or Romano cheese
1 tablespoon snipped fresh parsley
1 tablespoon finely chopped onion
½ teaspoon garlic salt
⅛ teaspoon black pepper
8 ounces lean ground beef
1 15-ounce can garbanzo beans (chickpeas), rinsed and drained
1 14-ounce can beef broth
1 14½-ounce can Italian-style stewed tomatoes, undrained
1½ cups water
1 cup sliced fresh mushrooms
1½ teaspoons dried Italian seasoning, crushed
¼ cup dried tiny bow tie pasta or ditalini
3 cups torn spinach or ½ of a 10-ounce package frozen chopped spinach, thawed and well drained
Finely shredded Parmesan or Romano cheese (optional)

1 In a medium bowl combine egg, bread crumbs, 2 tablespoons cheese, parsley, onion, garlic salt, and pepper. Add ground beef; mix well. Shape meat mixture into 36 balls using about 1 teaspoon of the meat mixture for each.

2 In a large skillet cook meatballs over medium heat about 8 minutes or until no longer pink, turning occasionally to brown evenly. Using a slotted spoon, remove meatballs from skillet; set aside.

3 In a large saucepan combine garbanzo beans, broth, undrained tomatoes, water, mushrooms, and Italian seasoning. Bring to boiling. Add pasta. Return to boiling; reduce heat. Simmer, covered, for 10 to 12 minutes or until pasta is tender. Stir in spinach and meatballs. Cook for 1 to 2 minutes more or just until spinach is wilted and meatballs are heated through. If desired, top with cheese.

Nutrition Facts per serving: 320 cal., 12 g total fat (4 g sat. fat), 93 mg chol., 1,162 mg sodium, 29 g carbo., 8 g fiber, 23 g pro.
Daily Values: 28% vit. A, 14% vit. C, 14% calcium, 29% iron

Chinese Beef and Noodle Soup

FAST

Stir-frying is a uniquely Chinese invention, but cooks everywhere love its quick-to-the-table qualities. Here, the technique speeds up soup making and keeps flavors fresh.

Start to finish: 25 minutes **Makes:** 6 servings (about 9 cups)

3¾ cups water
2 14-ounce cans beef broth
3 tablespoons reduced-sodium soy sauce
1 teaspoon sesame oil
1½ cups dried gemelli or penne (6 ounces)
8 ounces beef flank steak
4 teaspoons cooking oil
1 to 2 tablespoons grated fresh ginger
6 cloves garlic, minced
½ cup sliced green onions
½ to 1 teaspoon crushed red pepper
5 cups coarsely shredded bok choy

1 In large saucepan combine water, broth, soy sauce, and sesame oil. Bring to boiling. Add pasta. Return to boiling. Reduce heat; boil gently for 10 to 12 minutes or until the pasta is tender but firm.

2 Meanwhile, thinly slice steak across the grain into thin, bite-size strips. Pour cooking oil into a wok or large skillet. Preheat over medium-high heat. Stir-fry ginger and garlic for 15 seconds. Add the beef, green onions, and crushed red pepper. Stir-fry for 2 to 3 minutes or until beef reaches desired doneness. Remove meat mixture from wok; add meat and bok choy to saucepan. Heat through.

Nutrition Facts per serving: 229 cal., 7 g total fat (2 g sat. fat), 18 mg chol., 746 mg sodium, 26 g carbo., 1 g fiber, 14 g pro.
Daily Values: 10% vit. A, 20% vit. C, 6% calcium, 16% iron

fresh ginger forever

I always keep some fresh ginger in my freezer. Whole ginger lasts almost indefinitely when frozen. To freeze, place unpeeled ginger in a freezer bag; seal and freeze. There is no need to thaw before using; just grate or slice the fresh ginger while it is frozen and return the rest to the freezer. For short-term storage, whole ginger will stay fresh for 2 to 3 weeks in the refrigerator when wrapped loosely in a paper towel.

Deanna Nolin
Test Kitchen Home Economist

Italian Wedding Soup ♥ FAST

Orzo pasta, sometimes called "rosamarina," is a small rice-shaped pasta. If orzo is not available, substitute spaghetti or linguine that has been broken into ¼- to ½-inch pieces.

Prep: 5 minutes **Cook:** 25 minutes **Makes:** 4 servings (about 7½ cups)

12	ounces lean ground beef or lean ground lamb
1	small fennel bulb, chopped (about ⅔ cup)
1	medium onion, chopped (½ cup)
2	cloves garlic, minced
4	cups beef broth
2	cups water
1	teaspoon dried oregano, crushed
2	bay leaves
¼	teaspoon cracked black pepper
½	cup dried orzo pasta
4	cups shredded escarole, curly endive, and/or spinach
3	ounces Parmigiano-Reggiano or domestic Parmesan cheese with rind, cut into 4 wedges (optional)

1 In a large saucepan cook beef, fennel, onion, and garlic over medium-high heat about 5 minutes or until the meat is brown and vegetables are nearly tender, stirring occasionally. Drain fat, if necessary.

2 Add broth, water, oregano, bay leaves, and pepper. Bring to boiling; reduce heat. Simmer, covered, for 10 minutes. Remove bay leaves. If desired, reserve bay leaves for garnish.

3 Stir in orzo. Return to boiling; reduce heat to medium. Boil gently, uncovered, about 10 minutes or just until pasta is tender, stirring occasionally. Remove from heat; stir in escarole.

4 To serve, place a wedge of cheese in each of 4 soup bowls. Ladle hot soup into bowls. If desired, garnish with reserved bay leaves.*

Nutrition Facts per serving: 262 cal., 10 g total fat (4 g sat. fat), 54 mg chol., 873 mg sodium, 22 g carbo., 7 g fiber, 21 g pro.
Daily Values: 11% vit. A, 11% vit. C, 5% calcium, 18% iron

***Note:** Bay leaves contribute a wonderful flavor and aroma to recipes. However, they should be removed before eating. If using for garnish, do not eat.

Hamburger Soup ♥

This hearty soup makes a great take-along lunch for the office. If you have a microwave oven in your office, make the soup ahead and freeze in single-serving containers.

Prep: 20 minutes **Cook:** 20 minutes **Makes:** 8 servings (about 12½ cups)

1½ pounds lean ground beef
2 cups thinly sliced carrots
1 large onion, chopped
   (1 cup)
1 cup sliced celery
½ cup chopped green sweet
   pepper
1 clove garlic, minced
6 cups water
1 28-ounce can diced
   tomatoes, undrained
1 8-ounce can tomato sauce
½ cup quick-cooking barley
1 tablespoon instant beef
   bouillon granules
2 bay leaves
1 tablespoon snipped fresh
   oregano or 1 teaspoon
   dried oregano, crushed
¼ teaspoon black pepper
¼ teaspoon salt
   Fresh oregano sprigs
   (optional)

1 In a Dutch oven cook beef, carrots, onion, celery, sweet pepper, and garlic over medium heat until meat is brown and vegetables are tender. Drain well; return to Dutch oven.

2 Stir in water. Add undrained tomatoes, tomato sauce, barley, bouillon granules, bay leaves, snipped or dried oregano, black pepper, and salt. Bring to boiling; reduce heat. Simmer, covered, about 20 minutes or until barley is tender. Discard bay leaves. If desired, garnish with oregano sprigs.

Nutrition Facts per serving: 229 cal., 8 g total fat (3 g sat. fat), 54 mg chol., 746 mg sodium, 20 g carbo., 3 g fiber, 18 g pro.
Daily Values: 155% vit. A, 39% vit. C, 7% calcium, 15% iron

To Make Ahead: Prepare soup as directed; cool slightly. Pour soup into freezer containers. Seal and freeze for up to 3 months. To reheat the frozen soup in microwave oven, place it in a microwave-safe bowl. Cover with vented plastic wrap. Microwave on 70% power (medium-high) until hot, stirring occasionally. (Allow about 7 minutes for 1 cup frozen soup, 9 minutes for 1½ cups, 11 minutes for 2 cups, or 19 minutes for 3 cups.)

Italian Beef Soup FAST

Keep the ingredients on hand for this easy soup and you'll always be prepared to stir up a hearty supper. It makes a great lunch too.

Start to finish: 25 minutes **Makes:** 6 to 8 servings (about 9 cups)

1   pound lean ground beef
2   14-ounce cans beef broth
1   16-ounce package frozen pasta with broccoli, corn, and carrots in garlic-seasoned sauce
1   14½-ounce can diced tomatoes, undrained
1½ cups no-salt-added tomato juice
2   teaspoons dried Italian seasoning, crushed
¼   cup grated Parmesan cheese

1 In a Dutch oven cook ground beef over medium-high heat until brown. Drain fat, if necessary.

2 Stir in broth, pasta with mixed vegetables, undrained tomatoes, tomato juice, and Italian seasoning. Bring to boiling; reduce heat. Simmer, uncovered, about 10 minutes or until pasta and vegetables are tender. Ladle into soup bowls. Sprinkle each serving with Parmesan cheese.

Nutrition Facts per serving: 279 cal., 13 g total fat (6 g sat. fat), 56 mg chol., 827 mg sodium, 21 g carbo., 3 g fiber, 20 g pro.
Daily Values: 30% vit. A, 57% vit. C, 8% calcium, 17% iron

Tex-Mex Chili

Fresh jalapeño peppers ignite meaty chili. For a milder version, omit the jalapeños and add a can of diced mild chile peppers.

Prep: 20 minutes **Cook:** 8 to 10 hours **Makes:** 4 to 6 servings (about 8½ cups)

1 pound bulk pork sausage or ground beef

1 15-ounce can red kidney beans, rinsed and drained

1 cup chopped celery

1 large onion, chopped (1 cup)

½ cup chopped green sweet pepper

1 to 2 fresh jalapeño peppers, seeded and chopped (see tip, page 12)

1 14½-ounce can diced tomatoes, undrained

1 10-ounce can chopped tomatoes and green chile peppers, undrained

1 cup hot-style vegetable juice or vegetable juice

1 6-ounce can low-sodium tomato paste

2 cloves garlic, minced

3 to 4 teaspoons chili powder

½ teaspoon ground cumin

½ cup shredded cheddar cheese (2 ounces)

¼ to ⅓ cup dairy sour cream

1 In a large skillet cook the meat over medium-high heat until brown. Drain fat.

2 In a 3½- to 5-quart slow cooker combine cooked meat, beans, celery, onion, sweet pepper, and jalapeño peppers. Add both cans of undrained tomatoes, vegetable juice, tomato paste, garlic, chili powder, and cumin.

3 Cover and cook on low-heat setting for 8 to 10 hours or on high-heat setting for 4 to 5 hours. Ladle chili into bowls. Pass cheese and sour cream with chili.

Nutrition Facts per serving: 665 cal., 41 g total fat (18 g sat. fat), 85 mg chol., 1,432 mg sodium, 44 g carbo., 12 g fiber, 30 g pro.
Daily Values: 43% vit. A, 115% vit. C, 27% calcium, 25% iron

Chili with Cornmeal Dumplings

This chili is extra thick and spicy. For a milder chili, substitute two 14-ounce cans diced tomatoes for the cans of chopped tomatoes and green chile peppers. This will make a thinner chili too.

Prep: 25 minutes **Cook:** 20 minutes **Makes:** 4 servings (about 7 cups)

1 pound ground beef
1 large onion, chopped (1 cup)
½ cup chopped green sweet pepper
2 cloves garlic, minced
2 10-ounce cans chopped tomatoes and green chile peppers, undrained
1 15-ounce can dark red kidney beans, rinsed and drained
1 8-ounce can tomato sauce
½ cup water
1 teaspoon chili powder
½ teaspoon ground cumin
¼ teaspoon salt
¼ teaspoon black pepper
1 recipe Cheesy Cornmeal Dumplings
Dairy sour cream

1 In a large saucepan or Dutch oven cook ground beef, onion, sweet pepper, and garlic over medium heat until meat is brown and onion is tender. Drain fat.

2 Stir in undrained tomatoes, beans, tomato sauce, water, chili powder, cumin, salt, and black pepper. Bring to boiling; reduce heat. Simmer, uncovered, for 5 minutes.

3 Drop Cheesy Cornmeal Dumplings by tablespoonfuls onto simmering chili. Simmer, covered, for 15 to 20 minutes more or until a toothpick inserted into dumplings comes out clean. Spoon chili and dumplings into bowls and top with sour cream.

Cheesy Cornmeal Dumplings: In a medium bowl stir together ½ cup all-purpose flour, ½ cup shredded cheddar cheese (2 ounces), ½ cup yellow cornmeal, 1 teaspoon baking powder, and dash black pepper. In a small bowl combine 1 beaten egg, 2 tablespoons milk, and 2 tablespoons cooking oil; add to flour mixture. Stir with a fork just until moistened.

Nutrition Facts per serving: 646 cal., 31 g total fat (12 g sat. fat), 145 mg chol., 1,515 mg sodium, 58 g carbo., 10 g fiber, 40 g pro.
Daily Values: 37% vit. A, 56% vit. C, 28% calcium, 34% iron

Beef and Red Bean Chili

Chipotle peppers in adobo sauce are doubly delicious in this rich chili. The jalapeño is a direct hit of heat, while the adobo sauce is a slow burn.

Prep: 70 minutes **Cook:** 10 to 12 hours **Makes:** 6 servings (about 8½ cups)

1 cup dry red beans or dry kidney beans

6 cups water

2 pounds boneless beef chuck, cut into 1-inch cubes

1 large onion, coarsely chopped (1 cup)

1 tablespoon olive oil

1 15-ounce can tomato sauce

1 14½-ounce can diced tomatoes with mild chiles, undrained

1 14-ounce can beef broth

1 or 2 chipotle chile peppers in adobo sauce, finely chopped, plus 2 teaspoons adobo sauce

2 teaspoons dried oregano, crushed

1 teaspoon ground cumin

½ teaspoon salt

¼ cup snipped fresh cilantro

1 medium red sweet pepper, chopped

1 Rinse beans. In a large saucepan or Dutch oven combine beans and 6 cups water. Bring to boiling; reduce heat. Simmer, uncovered, for 10 minutes. Remove from heat. Cover and let stand for 1 hour. Drain and rinse beans.

2 Meanwhile, in a large skillet cook half of the beef and the onion in hot oil over medium-high heat until meat is brown. Transfer to a 3½- or 4-quart slow cooker. Repeat with remaining beef. Add tomato sauce, undrained tomatoes, broth, chipotle peppers and adobo sauce, oregano, cumin, and salt to the cooker; stir to combine. Stir beans into cooker.

3 Cover and cook on low-heat setting for 10 to 12 hours or on high-heat setting for 5 to 6 hours. Spoon into mugs or bowls. Top with cilantro and sweet pepper.

Conventional Method: Prepare beans as directed in Step 1, except use a 4- to 5-quart Dutch oven. Drain and rinse beans; set aside. Brown the beef and onion as in Step 2, except use the Dutch oven. Return all meat to pan. Add tomato sauce, undrained tomatoes, broth, chipotle peppers and adobo sauce, oregano, cumin, salt, and beans. Stir to combine. Bring to boiling; reduce heat. Simmer, covered, for 1½ to 2 hours or until meat and beans are tender. Serve as directed above.

Nutrition Facts per serving: 516 cal., 26 g total fat (9 g sat. fat), 98 mg chol., 1,162 mg sodium, 32 g carbo., 8 g fiber, 38 g pro.
Daily Values: 34% vit. A, 91% vit. C, 7% calcium, 34% iron

Italian Chili

Garbanzo beans, also known as chickpeas, appear frequently in Italian soups and stews. Their mild, nutty taste and firm texture lend a pleasing note to this chili.

Prep: 20 minutes **Cook:** 6 to 8 hours **Makes:** 6 to 8 servings (about 9½ cups)

1 pound lean ground beef
8 ounces bulk Italian
    sausage
1 large onion, chopped
    (1 cup)
1 cup chopped green sweet
    pepper
3 cloves garlic, minced
1 28-ounce can Italian-style
    tomatoes, cut up and
    undrained
1 15-ounce can garbanzo
    beans (chickpeas),
    rinsed and drained
1 15-ounce can red kidney
    beans, rinsed and
    drained
1 cup water
3 tablespoons
    Worcestershire sauce
2 to 3 tablespoons chili
    powder
2 teaspoons dried basil,
    crushed
2 teaspoons dried oregano,
    crushed
½ teaspoon bottled hot
    pepper sauce (optional)
¼ teaspoon salt
    Hot cooked rice
    Shredded cheddar cheese
    Dairy sour cream

1 In a large skillet cook beef, sausage, onion, sweet pepper, and garlic over medium-high heat until meat is brown and vegetables are tender. Drain fat.

2 In a 3½- or 4-quart slow cooker combine the meat mixture, undrained tomatoes, garbanzo beans, kidney beans, water, Worcestershire sauce, chili powder, basil, oregano, bottled hot pepper sauce (if desired), and salt.

3 Cover and cook on low-heat setting for 6 to 8 hours or on high-heat setting for 3 to 4 hours. Serve over hot cooked rice. Top with cheese and sour cream.

Nutrition Facts per serving: 633 cal., 26 g total fat (10 g sat. fat), 90 mg chol., 1,188 mg sodium, 67 g carbo., 13 g fiber, 38 g pro.
Daily Values: 29% vit. A, 68% vit. C, 22% calcium, 38% iron

Salsa Verde Beef Stew

Mexican-style stewed tomatoes, salsa, and tortillas lend the south-of-the-border accent to this slow cooker stew. Complete the meal with a festive salad of romaine, orange sections, and avocado slices.

Prep: 30 minutes **Cook:** 8 to 9 hours **Makes:** 6 servings (about 9 cups)

1½ pounds boneless beef chuck pot roast

1 tablespoon cooking oil

4 medium unpeeled potatoes, cut into 1-inch pieces

1 large onion, coarsely chopped (1 cup)

1 green sweet pepper, cut into ½-inch pieces

1 15- or 16-ounce can pinto beans, rinsed and drained

1 14½-ounce can Mexican-style stewed tomatoes, undrained

1 cup bottled mild or medium green salsa

2 cloves garlic, minced

1 teaspoon ground cumin

6 flour tortillas, warmed

1 Trim the fat from beef. Cut the beef into 1-inch pieces. In a large skillet brown beef, half at a time, in hot oil over medium-high heat.

2 In a 3½- to 5-quart slow cooker combine beef, potatoes, onion, sweet pepper, beans, undrained tomatoes, salsa, garlic, and cumin.

3 Cover and cook on low-heat setting for 8 to 9 hours or on high-heat setting for 5 to 6 hours. Serve stew with the warmed tortillas.

Nutrition Facts per serving: 465 cal., 12 g total fat (3 g sat. fat), 72 mg chol., 709 mg sodium, 56 g carbo., 8 g fiber, 33 g pro.
Daily Values: 4% vit. A, 51% vit. C, 11% calcium, 31% iron

Green Chile Stew

Beer, salsa, hominy, green chile peppers, and cilantro add hearty flavor to this Southwestern stew. For extra kick, use medium-hot green salsa instead of mild.

Prep: 15 minutes **Cook:** 1¾ hours **Makes:** 8 servings (about 12 cups)

- 2 pounds beef stew meat
- ¼ cup all-purpose flour
- ¼ cup butter
- 6 cloves garlic, minced
- 3 cups beef broth
- 1 12-ounce bottle dark beer or nonalcoholic beer
- 1 cup mild or medium-hot green salsa
- 2 tablespoons snipped fresh oregano or 2 teaspoons dried oregano, crushed
- 1 teaspoon ground cumin
- 3 medium potatoes, cubed (about 2 cups)
- 1 14½-ounce can hominy, drained
- 2 4½-ounce cans diced green chile peppers, drained
- 12 green onions, bias-sliced into 1-inch pieces
- ½ cup snipped fresh cilantro

1 Toss beef cubes with flour. In a 4- or 4½-quart Dutch oven brown the beef cubes, half at a time, in hot butter. Using a slotted spoon, remove meat from Dutch oven.

2 Add garlic to Dutch oven; cook for 1 minute. Stir in broth, beer, salsa, oregano, and cumin. Return meat to Dutch oven. Bring to boiling; reduce heat. Simmer, covered, about 1¼ hours or until meat is nearly tender. Add potatoes; simmer about 30 minutes more or until meat and potatoes are tender. Stir in hominy, chile peppers, green onions, and cilantro; heat through.

Nutrition Facts per serving: 392 cal., 16 g total fat (6 g sat. fat), 97 mg chol., 720 mg sodium, 28 g carbo., 1 g fiber, 32 g pro.
Daily Values: 15% vit. A, 49% vit. C, 7% calcium, 38% iron

Old-Time Beef Stew

Generations of families have gathered around dinner tables to savor stews such as this one. It's filled with chunks of fork-tender beef and a medley of vegetables in a rich brown gravy.

Prep: 35 minutes **Cook:** 2¾ hours **Makes:** 6 servings (about 11 cups)

1½ pounds boneless beef stew
    meat, cut into 1-inch
    cubes
2 tablespoons cooking oil
4 cups water
1 large onion, sliced
2 cloves garlic, minced
2 tablespoons
    Worcestershire sauce
1 tablespoon lemon juice
1 teaspoon sugar
1 teaspoon salt
½ teaspoon paprika
¼ teaspoon black pepper
⅛ teaspoon ground allspice
1 bay leaf
6 medium carrots, peeled
    and bias-sliced into
    ¾-inch chunks
4 medium potatoes, cut into
    1-inch chunks
1 pound small white onions,
    peeled and halved
½ cup cold water
¼ cup all-purpose flour
    Snipped fresh parsley
    (optional)

1 In an 8-quart Dutch oven cook all of the meat at once in hot oil over medium-high heat for 15 to 20 minutes or until the meat is brown, stirring occasionally. Drain fat. Add the 4 cups water, sliced onion, garlic, Worcestershire sauce, lemon juice, sugar, salt, paprika, pepper, allspice, and bay leaf to the Dutch oven. Bring to boiling; reduce heat. Simmer, covered, for 2 hours, stirring occasionally.

2 Stir in the carrots, potatoes, and halved onions. Return to boiling; reduce heat. Simmer, covered, about 30 minutes more or until meat and vegetables are tender. Discard bay leaf.

3 In a screw-top jar combine the ½ cup cold water and flour; cover and shake until smooth. Add flour mixture to stew. Cook and stir over medium heat until thickened and bubbly. Cook and stir for 1 minute more. Season to taste with salt and pepper. Spoon stew into bowls. If desired, sprinkle each serving with parsley.

Nutrition Facts per serving: 386 cal., 13 g total fat (4 g sat. fat), 61 mg chol., 561 mg sodium, 39 g carbo., 6 g fiber, 29 g pro.
Daily Values: 383% vit. A, 45% vit. C, 7% calcium, 26% iron

Beef Stew with Lentils

One pound of meat is enough to serve eight when you mix it with protein-rich lentils and lots of vegetables.

Prep: 20 minutes **Cook:** 1 hour **Makes:** 8 servings (about 11 cups)

1 pound boneless beef
    chuck steak or lamb
    stew meat
  Nonstick cooking spray
7 cups beef broth
1 large onion, chopped
    (1 cup)
1 cup sliced celery
1 cup sliced carrot
1½ cups lentils, rinsed and
    drained
1 14½-ounce can stewed
    tomatoes, undrained
1 bay leaf
1 9-ounce package frozen
    Italian-style green beans

1 Trim fat from meat; cut the meat into ½-inch pieces. Lightly coat a 4-quart Dutch oven with cooking spray. Cook the meat, half at a time, over medium-high heat until brown. Drain fat. Return all of the meat to the pan.

2 Add broth, onion, celery, and carrot. Bring to boiling; reduce heat. Simmer, uncovered, for 5 minutes. Add the lentils, undrained tomatoes, and bay leaf. Return to boiling; reduce heat. Simmer, uncovered, about 45 minutes or until lentils are tender and stew is thickened.

3 Add green beans. Return to boiling; reduce heat. Simmer, covered, about 10 minutes more or until beans are tender. Discard bay leaf.

Nutrition Facts per serving: 311 cal., 11 g total fat (4 g sat. fat), 37 mg chol., 863 mg sodium, 31 g carbo., 13 g fiber, 24 g pro.
Daily Values: 80% vit. A, 14 % vit. C, 6% calcium, 28% iron

Carbonnade of Beef and Vegetables

A carbonnade is a thick Belgian stew made with beef, beer, onions, and brown sugar. It's known for its rich, meaty flavor. Carrots and parsnips provide extra sweetness and a bit of color.

Prep: 15 minutes **Cook:** 1¼ hours **Makes:** 8 servings (about 8 cups)

4 slices bacon
2 pounds boneless beef top round steak, cut into 1-inch cubes
3 large leeks or medium onions, sliced
2 12-ounce bottles dark beer, ale, or nonalcoholic beer (3 cups)
¼ cup red wine vinegar
3 tablespoons brown sugar
2 tablespoons instant beef bouillon granules
4 cloves garlic, minced
2 teaspoons dried thyme, crushed
½ teaspoon black pepper
1½ pounds carrots and/or parsnips, peeled and bias-cut into ½-inch slices
¼ cup all-purpose flour
¼ cup cold water
Hot cooked wide noodles
Fresh thyme sprigs (optional)

1 In a 4-quart Dutch oven cook bacon until crisp. Remove bacon; drain on paper towels. Crumble bacon and set aside.

2 Brown the meat, half at a time, in hot bacon drippings in Dutch oven. Drain fat. Return all of the meat to the Dutch oven. Add leeks, beer, vinegar, brown sugar, bouillon granules, garlic, thyme, and pepper. Bring to boiling; reduce heat. Simmer, covered, for 45 minutes, stirring occasionally. Add carrots. Return to boiling; reduce heat. Simmer, covered, for 30 to 35 minutes more or until meat and vegetables are tender.

3 In a screw-top jar combine water and flour; cover and shake until smooth. Add flour mixture to meat mixture. Cook and stir over medium heat until thickened and bubbly. Cook and stir for 1 minute more. Stir in bacon. Serve over hot noodles. If desired, garnish with fresh thyme.

Nutrition Facts per serving: 390 cal., 6 g total fat (2 g sat. fat), 94 mg chol., 813 mg sodium, 42 g carbo., 4 g fiber, 33 g pro.
Daily Values: 385% vit. A, 12% vit. C, 6% calcium, 28% iron

To Make Ahead: Prepare as directed. Cool slightly. Chill or freeze in tightly covered containers. To reheat chilled stew, place in a saucepan; cook, covered, over medium-low heat for 10 to 15 minutes or until hot, stirring occasionally. For frozen stew, place the unthawed stew in a saucepan; cook, covered, over low heat for 45 to 50 minutes or until hot, stirring occasionally.

cleaning leeks

Prized by gourmets, leeks are more mellow than their cousins, onions and garlic. Before they're washed, they're also more gritty because their tightly packed leaves easily collect soil. To clean leeks, remove any outer leaves that have wilted. Slice the leek lengthwise in half, all the way through the root end. Holding the leek under a faucet with the root end up, rinse the leek under cold, running water, lifting and separating the leaves with your fingers to allow the grit to flow down through the top of the leek. Continue rinsing until all the grit is removed. Slice off the root end before using.

Hearty Rice and Sausage Soup

In this weeknight soup, quick-cooking rice not only cooks in minutes but also retains its shape and a pleasant firmness.

Prep: 20 minutes **Cook:** 25 minutes **Makes:** 4 servings (about 8 cups)

1 pound bulk pork sausage
   or turkey sausage
1 medium onion, chopped
   (½ cup)
½ cup coarsely chopped
   green sweet pepper
1 clove garlic, minced
2 cups water
1 14½-ounce can Mexican-
   style stewed tomatoes,
   undrained
1 10½-ounce can condensed
   beef broth
½ of a 6-ounce can tomato
   paste (⅓ cup)
½ teaspoon chili powder
3 cups quick-cooking rice
1 medium zucchini, halved
   lengthwise and sliced
   ¼ inch thick
   Dairy sour cream
   (optional)
   Broken tortilla chips
   (optional)

1 In a large saucepan or Dutch oven cook sausage, onion, sweet pepper, and garlic over medium heat until onion is tender and sausage is brown. Drain fat.

2 Stir water, undrained tomatoes, broth, tomato paste, and chili powder into sausage mixture. Bring to boiling; reduce heat. Add uncooked rice. Simmer, covered, for 5 minutes. Add zucchini and cook about 5 minutes more or until rice and zucchini are tender. Ladle soup into bowls. If desired, top with sour cream and tortilla chips.

Nutrition Facts per serving: 499 cal., 33 g total fat (13 g sat. fat), 65 mg chol., 1,499 mg sodium, 24 g carbo., 2 g fiber, 19 g pro.
Daily Values: 7% vit. A, 66% vit. C, 5% calcium, 12% iron

Curried Pumpkin Soup FAST

This creamy golden soup is rich with green onions, pumpkin, and ham. A touch of curry makes it even more mouthwatering. To reduce the saltiness, use low-sodium chicken broth and reduced-sodium ham.

Start to finish: 15 minutes **Makes:** 4 servings (about 7 cups)

¾ cup chopped green onion
1½ to 2 teaspoons curry
      powder
¼ cup butter
¼ cup all-purpose flour
1 15-ounce can pumpkin
2 cups chicken broth
2 cups buttermilk
1 cup cubed cooked ham
    Sliced green onion
      (optional)

1 In a 3-quart saucepan cook chopped green onion and curry powder in hot butter over medium heat 2 minutes or until onion is tender. Stir in flour. Add pumpkin and broth. Cook and stir until thickened and bubbly. Cook and stir 1 minute more.

2 Stir in buttermilk and ham; heat through. Ladle into soup bowls. If desired, top with sliced green onion.

Nutrition Facts per serving: 282 cal., 15 g total fat (9 g sat. fat), 55 mg chol., 1,121 mg sodium, 19 g carbo., 4 g fiber, 17 g pro.
Daily Values: 269% vit. A, 15% vit. C, 15% calcium, 18% iron

Ham and Vegetable Soup

Sink a spoon into this medley of ham, potatoes, spinach, and herbs. Snipped dill keeps the flavor springtime fresh.

Start to finish: 45 minutes **Makes:** 5 servings (about 8½ cups)

1   medium onion, chopped
    (½ cup)
2   cloves garlic, minced
1   tablespoon butter
4   cups water
6   ounces tiny new potatoes,
    cut into ¾-inch pieces
    (1¼ cups)
1   medium carrot, sliced
    (½ cup)
½   cup long grain rice
1½ teaspoons instant chicken
    bouillon granules
2   tablespoons snipped fresh
    dill or 1 teaspoon dried
    dillweed
¼   teaspoon ground white or
    black pepper
2   cups cubed cooked
    reduced-sodium or
    regular ham
    (10 ounces)
½   of a 10-ounce package
    fresh spinach, stems
    removed and leaves
    chopped (about
    3¼ cups, lightly packed)
1   cup half-and-half or light
    cream
    Fresh dill sprigs (optional)

1 In a 4-quart Dutch oven cook onion and garlic in hot butter over medium heat until tender. Add water, potatoes, carrot, rice, bouillon granules, dried dillweed (if using), and pepper. Bring to boiling; reduce heat. Simmer, covered, about 15 minutes or until rice and vegetables are tender.

2 Add ham, spinach, and fresh dill (if using). Return to boiling; reduce heat. Simmer, covered, for 1 to 2 minutes more or just until spinach begins to wilt. Stir in half-and-half; heat through but do not boil. If desired, garnish with fresh dill sprigs.

Nutrition Facts per serving: 288 cal., 13 g total fat (7 g sat. fat), 57 mg chol., 901 mg sodium, 26 g carbo., 4 g fiber, 17 g pro.
Daily Values: 97% vit. A, 24% vit. C, 10% calcium, 23% iron

New England Ham and Pea Soup

Slow-simmering soups like this one save busy cooks from last-minute preparations. And while the cook takes a few minutes to relax, the flavors deepen and meld together.

Prep: 25 minutes   **Cook:** 1 hour 20 minutes   **Makes:** 6 servings (9½ cups)

2   14-ounce cans reduced-sodium chicken broth
3   cups water
1   pound cooked boneless ham, cut into ½-inch cubes
1½ cups dry green split peas, rinsed and drained
1   large onion, chopped (1 cup)
2   cloves garlic, minced
2   bay leaves
½   teaspoon dried thyme, crushed
⅛   teaspoon black pepper
1   cup chopped carrot
1   cup chopped celery

1 In a 4-quart Dutch oven combine broth, water, ham, split peas, onion, garlic, bay leaves, thyme, and pepper. Bring to boiling; reduce heat. Simmer, covered, for 1 hour, stirring occasionally.

2 Stir in the carrot and celery. Return to boiling; reduce heat. Simmer, covered, for 20 to 30 minutes more or until the vegetables are tender. Discard bay leaves.

Nutrition Facts per serving: 342 cal., 10 g total fat (3 g sat. fat), 43 mg chol., 1,636 mg sodium, 37 g carbo., 14 g fiber, 27 g pro.
Daily Values: 116% vit. A, 10% vit. C, 6% calcium, 18% iron

Endive, Ham, and Bean Soup ♥ FAST

Curly endive, often mistaken for chicory, grows in loose heads with lacy, green-rimmed outer leaves that curl at the tips. It is used mainly in salads, but here it is cooked briefly and enjoyed in a tasty bean soup.

Start to finish: 25 minutes **Makes:** 4 servings (about 6 cups)

1 medium onion, chopped
  (½ cup)
1 medium carrot, chopped
1 stalk celery, chopped
2 cloves garlic, minced
1 tablespoon olive oil or
  cooking oil
4 cups reduced-sodium
  chicken broth
1 19-ounce can white kidney
  (cannellini) beans,
  rinsed and drained
⅔ cup chopped cooked ham
¾ teaspoon dried sage,
  crushed
3 cups shredded curly
  endive or Chinese
  cabbage

1 In a large saucepan cook onion, carrot, celery, and garlic in hot oil over medium heat until tender. Stir in broth, beans, ham, and sage.

2 Bring to boiling. Stir in curly endive; reduce heat. Simmer, covered, about 3 minutes or just until endive wilts.

Nutrition Facts per serving: 226 cal., 6 g total fat (1 g sat. fat), 13 mg chol., 1,281 mg sodium, 33 g carbo., 11 g fiber, 20 g pro.
Daily Values: 66% vit. A, 10% vit. C, 7% calcium, 18% iron

kitchen timesavers

I am always looking for ways to cut prep time in the kitchen. Here are a few of my timesaving tricks.

- If dry beans are called for in a recipe, consider reaching for a can of beans instead. You'll eliminate the time it takes to soak and cook the dried varieties.

- Assemble and measure your ingredients before starting to cook.

- Buy produce or meat and poultry that has already been cut to the appropriate size for your recipe.

- Leave the skins on potatoes when you use them in a soup that calls for sliced or chopped potatoes.

Marilyn Cornelius

Test Kitchen Home Economist

Bratwurst and Potato Soup

Slices of spicy bratwurst perk up creamy potato soup and transform this favorite side to main-dish status. A dash of bottled hot pepper sauce adds the right amount of heat.

Prep: 15 minutes **Cook:** 30 minutes **Makes:** 4 servings (about 5½ cups)

1 medium onion, chopped (½ cup)
½ cup shredded carrot
1 tablespoon butter
2 cups sliced potatoes (2 medium)
1½ cups chicken broth
1 cup milk
2 tablespoons all-purpose flour
12 ounces cooked bratwurst, sliced
½ cup frozen peas
Dash bottled hot pepper sauce

1 In a 3-quart saucepan cook onion and carrot in hot butter over medium heat about 4 minutes or until onion is tender. Add potatoes and broth. Bring to boiling; reduce heat. Simmer, covered, about 20 minutes or until potatoes are tender.

2 In a screw-top jar combine milk and flour; cover and shake until smooth. Stir flour mixture into potato mixture. Add bratwurst, peas, and hot pepper sauce. Cook and stir over medium heat until thickened and bubbly. Cook and stir for 1 minute more.

Nutrition Facts per serving: 425 cal., 27 g total fat (11 g sat. fat), 64 mg chol., 858 mg sodium, 26 g carbo., 3 g fiber, 19 g pro.
Daily Values: 84% vit. A, 30% vit. C, 14% calcium, 16% iron

Curried Split Pea Soup

Dried cranberries add color and tang to split pea soup. With its red and green color, this flavorful soup is perfect to serve on Christmas Eve.

Prep: 10 minutes **Cook:** 10 to 12 hours **Makes:** 6 servings (about 7½ cups)

1 pound dry green split
   peas, rinsed and drained
1 pound ham hocks
8 ounces cooked ham,
   cubed (1½ cups)
3 medium stalks celery,
   chopped (1½ cups)
1 large onion, chopped
   (1 cup)
2 medium carrots, chopped
   (1 cup)
2 bay leaves
⅓ cup dried cranberries
4 teaspoons curry powder
1 tablespoon dried
   marjoram, crushed
¼ teaspoon black pepper
6 cups water

1 In a 3½- or 4-quart slow cooker combine split peas, ham hocks, ham, celery, onion, carrots, bay leaves, cranberries, curry powder, marjoram, and pepper. Add water.

2 Cover and cook on low-heat setting for 10 to 12 hours or on high-heat setting for 5 to 6 hours. Discard bay leaves. Remove ham hocks. When cool enough to handle, remove meat from bones; discard bones. Coarsely chop meat. Return meat to soup.

Nutrition Facts per serving: 376 cal., 4 g total fat (1 g sat. fat), 25 mg chol., 626 mg sodium, 58 g carbo., 6 g fiber, 29 g pro.
Daily Values: 55% vit. A, 25% vit. C, 7% calcium, 34% iron

Lentil and Sausage Soup

Chorizo, a pork sausage popular in Latin dishes, is somewhat spicy. If you wish, substitute your favorite smoked sausage.

Prep: 15 minutes **Cook:** 40 minutes **Makes:** 4 servings (about 7 cups)

7 to 8 ounces cooked smoked chorizo or other cooked smoked sausage, sliced
1 tablespoon butter
1 cup thinly sliced carrot
1 cup sliced celery
1 cup chopped onion
2 cloves garlic, minced
2 14-ounce cans chicken broth
1 cup dry brown lentils, rinsed and drained
¼ to ½ teaspoon black pepper
4 cups hot cooked rice

1 In a large saucepan or Dutch oven cook sausage in hot butter over medium-high heat for 3 minutes. Add carrot, celery, onion, and garlic. Cook about 5 minutes more or just until vegetables are tender, stirring occasionally.

2 Carefully add broth, lentils, and pepper. Bring to boiling; reduce heat. Simmer, covered, about 30 minutes or until lentils are very tender, stirring occasionally. Serve with rice.

Nutrition Facts per serving: 676 cal., 25 g total fat (10 g sat. fat), 52 mg chol., 1,549 mg sodium, 81 g carbo., 18 g fiber, 32 g pro.
Daily Values: 105% vit. A, 12% vit. C, 7% calcium, 28% iron

types of lentils

Three types of lentils are commonly available: the brown lentil, which actually has a greenish brown coat and a yellow interior; the red lentil; and the yellow lentil. In food specialty stores, more exotic varieties such as green, white, or black also are available.

The brown lentil is the most widely used and called for in most of the recipes in this book. If you wish to substitute one type of lentil for another, you may need to adjust cooking times. Red lentils, for example, are significantly smaller than brown lentils, so you should reduce the cooking time. In the case of yellow lentils, which are the same size as the brown, cooking time should remain about the same. Check package labels for directions.

Pork and Mushroom Soup

Spend a little time putting this on the stove. Then you can relax and enjoy yourself, knowing that a meaty, veggie-packed supper is simmering to perfection.

Prep: 15 minutes **Cook:** 1 hour **Makes:** 4 servings (about 6½ cups)

1   pound pork stew meat, cut into 1-inch cubes
2   tablespoons butter
1   14-ounce can chicken broth
¼   cup dry white wine
3   tablespoons snipped fresh parsley
¾   teaspoon snipped fresh thyme or ¼ teaspoon dried thyme, crushed
¼   teaspoon garlic powder
⅛   teaspoon black pepper
1   bay leaf
2   cups frozen whole small onions
1   8-ounce package peeled baby carrots (2 cups)
1   4-ounce can whole mushrooms, drained
1   cup cold water
3   tablespoons all-purpose flour

1 In a large saucepan cook pork, half at a time, in hot butter over medium heat until brown. Return all of the meat to the saucepan. Stir in broth, wine, parsley, thyme, garlic powder, pepper, and bay leaf. Bring to boiling; reduce heat. Simmer, covered, for 40 minutes.

2 Add the frozen onions, carrots, and mushrooms. Return to boiling; reduce heat. Simmer, covered, about 20 minutes more or until vegetables are tender. Discard bay leaf.

3 In a screw-top jar combine cold water and flour; cover and shake until smooth. Add flour mixture to soup. Cook and stir over medium heat until thickened and bubbly. Cook and stir for 1 minute more.

Nutrition Facts per serving: 317 cal., 14 g total fat (6 g sat. fat), 90 mg chol., 605 mg sodium, 18 g carbo., 4 g fiber, 27 g pro.
Daily Values: 295% vit. A, 22% vit. C, 6% calcium, 16% iron

crushing dried herbs

You'll get more flavor out of dried herbs if you crush them before adding them to recipes. For the correct amount, first measure the herb in a measuring spoon, then empty the spoon into your hand. Crush the herb with the fingers of your other hand to release the herb's flavor and add it to the specified ingredients.

Some dried herbs, such as rosemary and thyme, are more easily crushed with a mortar and pestle—but if you don't have them, use a wooden spoon against the inside of a bowl.

Chunky Ham and Potato Chowder

Brimming with chunks of ham and potato, this hearty soup lives up to its name. Slightly mashing the potatoes thickens the chowder to a pleasing consistency.

Prep: 20 minutes **Cook:** 20 minutes **Makes:** 4 servings (about 4½ cups)

3 medium potatoes, peeled and diced

1 small leek, sliced, or 1 small onion, chopped

1 cup chicken broth

2 cups milk

1 tablespoon butter

½ teaspoon snipped fresh thyme or ⅛ teaspoon dried thyme, crushed

¼ teaspoon ground black pepper

1½ cups diced fully cooked ham or diced smoked turkey

1 tablespoon snipped fresh basil leaves (optional)

Cracked black pepper

1 In a 2-quart saucepan combine potatoes, leek, and broth. Bring to boiling; reduce heat. Simmer, covered, about 15 minutes or until potatoes are tender. Mash slightly.

2 Add milk, butter, thyme, ground black pepper, ham, and, if desired, basil. Heat through. Ladle into bowls; sprinkle with cracked pepper.

Nutrition Facts per serving: 262 cal., 11 g total fat (5 g sat. fat), 47 mg chol., 959 mg sodium, 24 g carbo., 1 g fiber, 16 g pro.
Daily Values: 8% vit. A, 24% vit. C, 17% calcium, 8% iron

Corny Sausage Chowder

This thick and creamy chowder makes a satisfying supper. Finish off the meal with a tossed green salad and slices of your favorite bakery bread.

Start to finish: 50 minutes **Makes:** 6 servings (about 10 cups)

1 pound bulk pork sausage
1 medium onion, chopped (½ cup)
3 medium potatoes, peeled and cut into ½-inch cubes
2 cups water
1 teaspoon dried basil or Italian seasoning, crushed
½ teaspoon black pepper
1 15¼-ounce can whole kernel corn, drained
1 14¾-ounce can cream-style corn
1 12-ounce can (1½ cups) evaporated milk

1 In a 4-quart Dutch oven cook sausage over medium-high heat for 5 minutes. Add onion; cook about 5 minutes more or until sausage is brown and onion is tender.

2 Add potatoes, water, basil, and pepper. Bring to boiling; reduce heat. Simmer, covered, about 20 minutes or until potatoes are tender.

3 Stir in the whole kernel corn, cream-style corn, and evaporated milk. Heat through.

Nutrition Facts per serving: 436 cal., 22 g total fat (3 g sat. fat), 19 mg chol., 408 mg sodium, 38 g carbo., 4 g fiber, 20 g pro.
Daily Values: 5% vit. A, 19% vit. C, 21% calcium, 17% iron

Creamy Ham and Vegetable Stew ♥

Canned soup and processed cheese dip provide this easy stew with a velvety texture. Serve it with slices of rye or pumpernickel bread.

Start to finish: 35 minutes **Makes:** 4 servings (about 6½ cups)

1½ cups water
2 carrots, peeled and cut into 1-inch pieces
1 cup diced, peeled potato (1 medium)
1 medium onion, cut into chunks
1 cup frozen peas
1 cup cubed cooked ham
1 10¾-ounce can condensed reduced-sodium cream of celery soup
½ of an 8-ounce jar process cheese dip (½ cup)

1 In a large saucepan combine the water, carrots, potato, and onion. Bring to boiling; reduce heat. Simmer, covered, for 10 minutes.

2 Add peas and ham. Return to boiling; reduce heat. Simmer, covered, for 5 minutes more. Stir in soup and cheese dip. Cook and stir until heated.

Nutrition Facts per serving: 257 cal., 11 g total fat (5 g sat. fat), 40 mg chol., 1,248 mg sodium, 27 g carbo., 4 g fiber, 13 g pro.
Daily Values: 164% vit. A, 23% vit. C, 11% calcium, 8% iron

the right temperature

To keep soups and stews warm longer, I warm the bowls before dishing up the soup. Rinse the bowls under hot tap water and dry before filling them with soup. Likewise, if you're serving a cold soup, chill the bowls in the refrigerator before dishing up.

Lori Wilson
Test Kitchen Home Economist

Gingersnap Stew

Crushed gingersnaps provide the thickening, as well as a piquant flavor, in this zesty sausage and bean stew.

Prep: 20 minutes **Cook:** 25 minutes **Makes:** 4 servings (about 5½ cups)

3 carrots, cut into ¾-inch pieces
3 medium stalks celery, cut into ½-inch pieces
¼ cup chopped onion
2 teaspoons cooking oil
8 ounces cooked smoked sausage, halved lengthwise and cut into 1-inch pieces
1½ cups water
½ of a 15-ounce can kidney beans, rinsed and drained
1 tablespoon chili powder
1 tablespoon Worcestershire sauce
1 14½-ounce can stewed tomatoes, undrained
6 gingersnaps, crushed (about ⅓ cup)
Pumpernickel bread (optional)

1 In a large saucepan cook carrots, celery, and onion in hot oil over medium heat about 5 minutes or until onion is nearly tender. Remove vegetables from pan and set aside.

2 Add sausage to pan. Cook over medium heat until light brown. Return vegetables to pan. Add water, beans, chili powder, and Worcestershire sauce. Bring to boiling; reduce heat. Simmer, covered, about 20 minutes or until the vegetables are tender.

3 Stir in undrained tomatoes. Add crushed gingersnaps. Cook and stir over medium heat about 5 minutes or until mixture is thickened and bubbly. Ladle into bowls. If desired, serve with pumpernickel bread.

Nutrition Facts per serving: 410 cal., 23 g total fat (7 g sat. fat), 39 mg chol., 1,302 mg sodium, 35 g carbo., 7 g fiber, 19 g pro.
Daily Values: 302% vit. A, 19% vit. C, 11% calcium, 19% iron

Pork and Orzo Soup with Spinach

Boneless pork chops are an easy-to-handle choice for soups. The pasta, fresh herbs, and spinach add a Mediterranean character to this meaty soup.

Start to finish: 50 minutes **Makes:** 6 servings (about 10½ cups)

1½ pounds boneless pork loin chops, cut into 1-inch cubes

2 tablespoons cooking oil

4 cups water

2 14-ounce cans chicken broth or vegetable broth

2 bay leaves

1 tablespoon snipped fresh oregano or 1 teaspoon dried oregano, crushed

1½ teaspoons snipped fresh marjoram or ½ teaspoon dried marjoram, crushed

½ teaspoon salt

¼ teaspoon black pepper

2 carrots, cut into julienne strips (1 cup)

1 cup sliced celery

¾ cup dried orzo pasta (rosamarina)

3 cups torn spinach or half of a 10-ounce package frozen chopped spinach, thawed and well drained

1 In a 4-quart Dutch oven cook the meat, half at a time, in hot oil over medium-high heat until brown. Drain the fat.

2 Stir in water, broth, bay leaves, oregano, marjoram, salt, and pepper. Bring to boiling. Stir in carrots, celery, and pasta. Return to boiling; reduce heat. Simmer, covered, about 15 minutes or until the vegetables and pasta are tender. Discard bay leaves.

3 Stir in spinach. Cook for 1 to 2 minutes more or just until spinach wilts.

Nutrition Facts per serving: 261 cal., 9 g total fat (3 g sat. fat), 62 mg chol., 709 mg sodium, 13 g carbo., 3 g fiber, 30 g pro.
Daily Values: 121% vit. A, 11% vit. C, 6% calcium, 17% iron

Lamb, Lentil, and Onion Soup ♥

This soup gets a flavor boost from thyme. For optimum flavor, make sure the dried thyme you use still has plenty of fragrance. If not, it's time to buy a replacement.

Prep: 25 minutes **Cook:** 7 to 8 hours **Makes:** 4 or 5 servings (about 9½ cups)

12 ounces lean boneless lamb or beef, cut into ½-inch cubes
1 tablespoon cooking oil
1 cup thinly sliced celery
1 cup coarsely chopped carrot
1 cup dry lentils, rinsed and drained
1 10½-ounce can condensed French onion soup
1 to 1½ teaspoons dried thyme, crushed
¼ teaspoon black pepper
3¼ cups water

1 In a large skillet brown meat in hot oil over medium-high heat. Meanwhile, in a 3½- or 4-quart slow cooker place celery, carrot, and lentils. Top with browned meat.

2 In a large bowl combine soup, thyme, and pepper. Gradually stir in water. Add soup mixture to slow cooker.

3 Cover and cook on low-heat setting for 7 to 8 hours or on high-heat setting for 3½ to 4 hours.

Nutrition Facts per serving: 376 cal., 10 g total fat (2 g sat. fat), 57 mg chol., 693 mg sodium, 38 g carbo., 17 g fiber, 33 g pro.
Daily Values: 156% vit. A, 12% vit. C, 7% calcium, 33% iron

Lamb Stew with Sweet Potatoes

A delightful blend of spices, inspired by the cuisines of the Middle East, combines deliciously with lamb and dried fruit. Serve the tantalizing result over mashed sweet potatoes.

Prep: 30 minutes **Cook:** 1½ hours **Makes:** 6 servings (about 7 cups)

2 pounds lamb stew meat, cut into 1-inch cubes
¼ teaspoon salt
¼ teaspoon black pepper
2 tablespoons cooking oil
2 tablespoons all-purpose flour
2 14-ounce cans vegetable broth
1 12-ounce can apricot or mango nectar
1 2-inch stick cinnamon or ¼ teaspoon ground cinnamon
3 cloves garlic, minced
½ teaspoon ground cumin
½ teaspoon ground cardamom
⅛ teaspoon thread saffron, crushed
3 medium carrots, cut into ½-inch pieces (1½ cups)
1½ cups frozen pearl onions
1 cup dried apricots
1 cup dried pitted plums (prunes)
1 recipe Mashed Sweet Potatoes
Fresh sage leaves (optional)

1 Season lamb with salt and pepper. In a 4-quart Dutch oven brown meat, half at a time, in hot oil over medium-high heat. Drain fat. Return all meat to pan. Sprinkle meat with flour, stirring to coat. Add broth, nectar, cinnamon, garlic, cumin, cardamom, and saffron; stir to combine. Bring to boiling; reduce heat. Simmer, covered, for 1 hour or until meat is nearly tender.

2 Add carrots, onions, apricots, and plums. Return to boiling; reduce heat. Simmer, covered, about 30 minutes more or until vegetables are tender. Remove stick cinnamon (if using). Serve over Mashed Sweet Potatoes or your favorite mashed potatoes. If desired, garnish with sage.

Mashed Sweet Potatoes: Peel and quarter 2 pounds sweet potatoes. In a large saucepan cook potatoes, covered, in a moderate amount of lightly salted boiling water for 20 to 25 minutes or until tender; drain. Mash with a potato masher or beat with an electric mixer on low speed. Add ¼ cup butter, cut up, and ¼ cup plain yogurt; beat or mash until smooth. If necessary, stir in a little milk to reach desired consistency.

Nutrition Facts per serving: 613 cal., 20 g total fat (7 g sat. fat), 117 mg chol., 881 mg sodium, 80 g carbo., 10 g fiber, 36 g pro.
Daily Values: 730% vit. A, 59% vit. C, 12% calcium, 32% iron

Cassoulet-Style Stew

Based on a classic French dish, this full-flavored stew is perfect for casual entertaining. Its slow simmering allows the cook plenty of time to relax and converse with guests.

Prep: 50 minutes **Stand:** 1 hour **Cook:** 1¾ hours **Makes:** 6 servings (about 9½ cups)

8 ounces dry navy beans
3 cups water
1 meaty lamb shank (1 to 1½ pounds)
1 tablespoon olive oil or cooking oil
1 cup chopped celery (including leaves)
1 medium potato, peeled and coarsely chopped
½ cup coarsely chopped peeled carrot
½ cup coarsely chopped peeled parsnip
2 cloves garlic, minced
3½ cups water
1½ cups sliced fresh mushrooms
⅔ cup dry black-eyed peas, rinsed and drained
¼ cup dry red wine or beef broth
1¼ teaspoons salt
1 tablespoon snipped fresh thyme or 1 teaspoon dried thyme, crushed
2 teaspoons snipped fresh rosemary or ½ teaspoon dried rosemary, crushed
¼ teaspoon black pepper
1 14½-ounce can diced tomatoes, drained
Fresh rosemary or thyme sprigs (optional)

1 Rinse beans. In a Dutch oven combine beans and the 3 cups water. Bring to boiling; reduce heat. Simmer, uncovered, for 2 minutes. Remove from heat. Cover and let stand for 1 hour. (Or place beans in water in a Dutch oven. Cover and let stand in a cool place for 6 to 8 hours or overnight.) Drain and rinse beans.

2 In a 4- to 5-quart Dutch oven brown lamb shank in hot oil over medium-high heat. Add celery, potato, carrot, parsnip, and garlic. Cook for 5 minutes, stirring frequently. Add the 3½ cups water, the mushrooms, black-eyed peas, wine, salt, dried thyme (if using), dried rosemary (if using), pepper, and beans. Bring to boiling; reduce heat. Simmer, covered, about 1½ hours or until the beans and peas are tender. Remove shank; let cool.

3 Remove meat from shank; chop meat. Stir meat, tomatoes, snipped fresh thyme (if using), and snipped fresh rosemary (if using) into bean mixture. Return to boiling; reduce heat. Simmer, covered, for 15 minutes more. To serve, ladle stew into bowls. If desired, garnish with fresh rosemary or thyme sprigs.

Nutrition Facts per serving: 310 cal., 8 g total fat (2 g sat. fat), 35 mg chol., 654 mg sodium, 39 g carbo., 12 g fiber, 20 g pro.
Daily Values: 54% vit. A, 28% vit. C, 13% calcium, 21% iron

To Make Ahead: Prepare stew as directed. Let cool for 30 minutes. Place stew in freezer containers and freeze for up to 3 months. To serve, place frozen stew in a saucepan. Heat, covered, over medium-low heat about 45 minutes or until heated through, stirring occasionally.

Lamb Stew with Couscous

In Middle Eastern countries, simple stews such as this one are made extraordinary with touches of sweetness from fruits and spices. Lamb, seasoned with garlic, cumin, and lemon, is a favorite meat.

Prep: 15 minutes **Cook:** 1¼ hours **Makes:** 4 servings (about 8 cups)

1   pound lamb stew meat, cut into ¾-inch cubes
2   tablespoons olive oil or cooking oil
2½ cups beef broth
1   8-ounce can tomato sauce
1   large onion, cut into wedges
2   medium carrots, sliced
1   tablespoon lemon juice
1   clove garlic, minced
¾   teaspoon ground cumin
½   teaspoon ground turmeric
¼   teaspoon salt
¼   teaspoon black pepper
1   small eggplant (about 1 pound), peeled and cut into ¾-inch cubes (4 cups)
1   large red sweet pepper, coarsely chopped
¼   cup raisins
⅓   cup cold water
3   tablespoons all-purpose flour
3   cups hot cooked couscous

1 In a Dutch oven brown meat, half at a time, in hot oil over medium-high heat. Drain fat. Stir in broth, tomato sauce, onion wedges, carrots, lemon juice, garlic, cumin, turmeric, salt, and black pepper. Bring to boiling; reduce heat. Simmer, covered, for 30 minutes.

2 Stir in eggplant, red sweet pepper, and raisins. Bring to boiling; reduce heat. Simmer, covered, about 30 minutes more or until meat and vegetables are tender. If necessary, skim fat from stew.

3 In a screw-top jar combine water and flour; cover and shake until smooth. Add flour mixture to stew. Cook and stir over medium heat until thickened and bubbly. Cook and stir for 1 minute more. Serve stew with hot cooked couscous.

Nutrition Facts per serving: 475 cal., 13 g total fat (3 g sat. fat), 57 mg chol., 1,045 mg sodium, 62 g carbo., 12 g fiber, 29 g pro.
Daily Values: 109% vit. A, 85% vit. C, 29% iron

Beef Ragout

Oxtails, the tails of beef or veal, give a special richness and flavor to this fortifying stew. The bony meat is available in the meat section of most supermarkets and requires long, slow cooking.

Prep: 30 minutes **Cook:** 1½ hours **Makes:** 5 or 6 servings (about 10 cups)

1 pound oxtails, cut into 1½- to 2-inch pieces (optional)

1 pound boneless beef short ribs (if omitting oxtails, use an additional ¼ pound boneless beef short ribs)

2 tablespoons cooking oil

2 14-ounce cans beef broth (about 3½ cups)

½ cup dry red wine or beef broth

½ cup coarsely chopped shallots

4 cloves garlic, minced

2 bay leaves

½ teaspoon salt

¼ to ½ teaspoon coarsely ground black pepper

1 pound carrots, peeled and cut into ¾-inch pieces

1 pound rutabagas or turnips, peeled and cut into ¾-inch cubes (about 3 cups)

2 medium onions, peeled and coarsely chopped (1 cup)

⅔ cup cold water

⅓ cup all-purpose flour

⅓ cup snipped fresh parsley

Hot cooked couscous (optional)

Cooked and crumbled bacon (optional)

Italian flat-leaf parsley (optional)

1 In a Dutch oven cook oxtails and ribs on all sides in hot oil over medium-high heat until brown. Drain fat. Carefully add the broth, wine, shallots, garlic, bay leaves, salt, and pepper to meat in Dutch oven. Bring to boiling; reduce heat. Simmer, covered, about 1 hour or until meat is nearly tender.

2 Add carrots, rutabagas, and onions. Return to boiling; reduce heat. Simmer, covered, for 30 to 45 minutes more or until meat and vegetables are tender. Discard bay leaves. Remove meat; cool slightly.

3 Meanwhile, in a screw-top jar combine cold water and flour; cover and shake until smooth. Add flour mixture to meat mixture. Cook and stir over medium heat until thickened and bubbly. Cook and stir for 1 minute more.

4 Cut meat into bite-size pieces, discarding any bones. Return meat to Dutch oven; heat through. Stir in snipped parsley. Season to taste with additional salt and pepper. If desired, serve with hot cooked couscous and sprinkle with bacon and parsley.

Nutrition Facts per serving: 441 cal., 27 g total fat (11 g sat. fat), 53 mg chol., 881 mg sodium, 28 g carbo., 6 g fiber, 18 g pro.
Daily Values: 227% vit. A, 48% vit. C, 8% calcium, 24% iron

Seafood

Red Pepper and Snapper Soup

In This Chapter:

Cajun Fish Soup 89
Caribbean Seafood Stew 112
Carolina Catfish Stew 114
Chunky Vegetable-
    Cod Soup 93
Country Fish Stew 118
Creamy Shrimp and
    Spinach Stew 111
Effortless Shrimp
    Chowder, 109
Fish Soup Provençale 90
Fish Stock 88

Italian Fish and
    Vegetable Soup 91
Lemon and Scallop Soup 97
Maryland Crab and
    Corn Chowder 108
Moroccan Bouillabaisse 117
North Sea Chowder 105
Paella Soup 95
Pearl-of-an-Oyster Stew 115
Red Pepper and
    Snapper Soup 92
Red Seafood Chowder 106
Roasted Corn and
    Crab Soup 96

Salmon Confetti Chowder 110
Salmon Pan Chowder 107
Sherried Salmon Bisque 103
Shrimp and
    Coconut Soup 100
Shrimp and Greens Soup 102
Shrimp-Tortilla Soup 98
Spicy Corn Chowder 104
Spicy Mexican-Style
    Fish Stew 116
Thai-Style Shrimp Soup 94

Fish Stock ♥

Homemade fish stock imparts superb richness to recipes, making it well worth the extra effort. You can use this stock in any fish or seafood recipe that calls for chicken or other broth.

Prep: 25 minutes **Cook:** 1 hour **Cool:** 30 minutes **Makes:** about 7 cups

3 pounds fresh or frozen
  fish heads and tails or
  drawn lean fish (cod,
  pike, flounder, haddock,
  hake, orange roughy, or
  porgy)
8 cups water
1 medium yellow onion, cut
  into wedges
¼ cup lemon juice
2 stalks celery with leaves,
  cut up
3 cloves garlic, halved
1 tablespoon grated fresh
  ginger or 1 teaspoon
  ground ginger
1 tablespoon dried
  marjoram, crushed
½ teaspoon dry mustard
½ teaspoon salt

1 Thaw fish, if frozen; rinse. Place fish in a 6-quart kettle or Dutch oven. Add water, onion, lemon juice, celery, garlic, ginger, marjoram, mustard, and salt. Bring to boiling; reduce heat. Simmer, covered, for 1 hour. Remove from heat; cool for 30 minutes.

2 Strain stock (see page 5). Discard fish, vegetables, and seasonings. If desired, clarify stock (see tip, page 8). Cover and chill for up to 2 days or freeze for up to 6 months.

Nutrition Facts per 1 cup: 1 cal., 174 mg sodium
Daily Values: 3% vit. C, 1% calcium

buying and storing

When buying fish look for signs that it is fresh. Fresh fish should have a mild scent and moist flesh, and appear newly cut. Don't purchase fish that has a strong, fishy odor. Frozen fish should meet the same fresh-smell test and have taut packaging with no evidence of ice or blood. Fresh fish is best used right away. Or you can store it for up to two days in the coldest part of your refrigerator. Frozen fish will keep in its original packaging, frozen at 0° or cooler, for up to 3 months.

Cajun Fish Soup ♥ FAST

This tongue-tingling soup gets its spirited flavor from Cajun seasoning. Several brands are available, and each differs slightly, but most include garlic, dried chiles, black pepper, and mustard.

Start to finish: 25 minutes **Makes:** 4 servings (about 7½ cups)

12 ounces fresh or frozen fish fillets or peeled and deveined shrimp

1 14-ounce can vegetable broth or chicken broth

1 cup sliced fresh mushrooms

1 small yellow summer squash or zucchini, halved lengthwise and sliced

1 medium onion, chopped (½ cup)

1 clove garlic, minced

1 to 1½ teaspoons Cajun seasoning

2 14½-ounce cans reduced-sodium stewed tomatoes, undrained

2 tablespoons snipped fresh oregano

½ teaspoon finely shredded lemon peel

1 Thaw the fish or shrimp, if frozen. If using fish, cut into 1-inch pieces; set aside.

2 In a large saucepan or Dutch oven combine broth, mushrooms, squash, onion, garlic, and Cajun seasoning. Bring to boiling; reduce heat. Simmer, covered, about 5 minutes or until the vegetables are tender.

3 Stir in the fish or shrimp and undrained tomatoes. Bring to boiling; reduce heat. Simmer, covered, for 2 to 3 minutes or until the fish flakes easily when tested with a fork or the shrimp turn pink. Remove from heat. Stir in oregano and lemon peel.

Nutrition Facts per serving: 149 cal., 2 g total fat (0 g sat. fat), 40 mg chol., 608 mg sodium, 20 g carbo., 5 g fiber, 17 g pro.
Daily Values: 18% vit. A, 32% vit. C, 4% calcium, 9% iron

Fish Soup Provençale ♥ FAST

The sweet essence of fresh fennel blends with fish, tomatoes, garlic, onion, and orange to create a soup reminiscent of the south of France.

Start to finish: 30 minutes **Makes:** 4 servings (about 8 cups)

8 ounces fresh or frozen skinless haddock, grouper, or halibut fillets

1 small fennel bulb

3 cups vegetable broth, Fish Stock (see recipe, page 88), or chicken broth

1 large onion, finely chopped (1 cup)

1 small yellow summer squash, cubed (about 1 cup)

1 cup dry white wine

1 teaspoon finely shredded orange or lemon peel

3 cloves garlic, minced

2 cups chopped fresh tomatoes or one 14½-ounce can diced tomatoes

2 tablespoons snipped fresh thyme

1 Thaw fish, if frozen. Cut fish into 1-inch pieces; set aside.

2 Cut off and discard upper stalks of fennel. Remove any wilted outer layers; cut a thin slice from base. Wash fennel; cut in half lengthwise and thinly slice.

3 In a large saucepan combine fennel, broth, onion, squash, wine, orange peel, and garlic. Bring to boiling; reduce heat. Simmer, covered, for 10 minutes. Stir in fish, tomatoes, and thyme. Return to boiling; reduce heat. Simmer, covered, about 3 minutes more or until fish flakes easily when tested with a fork. If desired, garnish with additional snipped thyme.

Nutrition Facts per serving: 156 cal., 3 g total fat (0 g sat. fat), 18 mg chol., 752 mg sodium, 15 g carbo., 8 g fiber, 14 g pro.
Daily Values: 11% vit. A, 46% vit. C, 6% calcium, 16% iron

Italian Fish and Vegetable Soup ♥

Any fan of Italian cooking knows that Italy can claim many great soups. And fish soups are among the best. When you're in the mood for a taste of Italy, try this rosemary-scented dish.

Start to finish: 35 minutes **Makes:** 4 servings (about 7½ cups)

12   ounces fresh or frozen sea bass, haddock, or cod fillets
3¼   cups water
1   14½-ounce can diced tomatoes, undrained
1½   cups packaged shredded cabbage with carrot (coleslaw mix)
1   small zucchini, chopped (about 1 cup)
1   stalk celery, chopped
1   small onion, chopped
¼   cup dry white wine or water
2   teaspoons instant chicken bouillon granules
2   teaspoons snipped fresh rosemary
2   bay leaves
2   cloves garlic, minced
¼   cup tomato paste

1 Thaw fish, if frozen. Cut into 1-inch pieces; set aside.

2 In a large saucepan combine water, undrained tomatoes, cabbage mix, zucchini, celery, onion, wine, bouillon granules, rosemary, bay leaves, and garlic. Bring to boiling; reduce heat. Simmer, covered, 10 minutes or until vegetables are crisp-tender.

3 Stir in tomato paste; add fish. Return to boiling; reduce heat. Simmer, covered, about 5 minutes more or until fish flakes easily when tested with a fork. Discard bay leaves.

Nutrition Facts per serving: 153 cal., 1 g total fat (0 g sat. fat), 49 mg chol., 825 mg sodium, 15 g carbo., 4 g fiber, 19 g pro.
Daily Values: 52% vit. A, 65% vit. C, 8% calcium, 17% iron

Red Pepper and Snapper Soup ♥

When you need a no-fail main dish, rely on this rich-tasting, easy-to-assemble fish soup. If red snapper is hard to come by, try it with cod or haddock.

Start to finish: 50 minutes **Makes:** 5 servings (about 9 cups)

1¼ pounds fresh or frozen skinless red snapper or other firm-fleshed fish fillets

3 medium red sweet peppers, coarsely chopped (2¼ cups)

1 cup chopped shallots or onions

2 tablespoons olive oil

3 14-ounce cans reduced-sodium chicken broth (5¼ cups total)

¼ teaspoon salt

¼ teaspoon ground black pepper

⅛ teaspoon ground red pepper

½ cup snipped fresh Italian flat-leaf parsley

Fresh Italian flat-leaf parsley sprigs (optional)

1 Thaw fish, if frozen. Rinse fish; pat dry. Cut fish into 1-inch pieces; set aside.

2 In a large saucepan or Dutch oven cook sweet peppers and shallots in hot oil over medium heat for 5 minutes. Carefully add 1 can of the broth. Bring to boiling; reduce heat. Simmer, covered, about 20 minutes or until peppers are very tender. Remove from heat; cool slightly.

3 Place half of the sweet pepper mixture in a blender container or food processor bowl. Cover and blend or process until nearly smooth. Repeat with remaining pepper mixture. Return all of the mixture to saucepan.

4 Add remaining broth, the salt, black pepper, and ground red pepper. Bring to boiling; reduce heat. Add fish to broth mixture. Simmer, covered, about 5 minutes or until fish flakes easily when tested with a fork, stirring once or twice. Stir in snipped parsley. If desired, garnish soup with parsley sprigs.

Nutrition Facts per serving: 223 cal., 8 g total fat (1 g sat. fat), 42 mg chol., 859 mg sodium, 10 g carbo., 0 g fiber, 27 g pro.
Daily Values: 76% vit. A, 142% vit. C, 5% calcium, 8% iron

Chunky Vegetable-Cod Soup

This colorful fish soup will win your family's approval—hook, line, and sinker! Serve it with a loaf of sourdough bread and an assortment of fresh fruit.

Prep: 20 minutes **Cook:** 13 minutes **Makes:** 4 servings (about 6½ cups)

1 pound fresh or frozen skinless cod fillets
½ cup chopped red sweet pepper
¼ cup chopped onion
1 tablespoon butter
2 14-ounce cans vegetable broth or chicken broth
1 cup frozen cut green beans
1 cup coarsely chopped cabbage
½ cup sliced carrot
1 teaspoon snipped fresh basil or ¼ teaspoon dried basil, crushed
1 teaspoon snipped fresh thyme or ¼ teaspoon dried thyme, crushed
½ teaspoon snipped fresh rosemary or ⅛ teaspoon dried rosemary, crushed
¼ teaspoon black pepper
Lemon wedges (optional)

1 Thaw fish, if frozen. Cut fish into 1-inch pieces. Set aside.

2 In a large saucepan or Dutch oven cook sweet pepper and onion in hot butter over medium heat until tender. Stir in broth, green beans, cabbage, carrot, basil, thyme, rosemary, and black pepper. Bring to boiling; reduce heat. Simmer, covered, for 8 to 10 minutes or until vegetables are nearly tender.

3 Add fish to saucepan. Return to boiling; reduce heat. Simmer, covered, about 5 minutes or until fish flakes easily when tested with a fork, stirring once. If desired, serve with lemon.

Nutrition Facts per serving: 168 cal., 5 g total fat (2 g sat. fat), 57 mg chol., 917 mg sodium, 10 g carbo., 2 g fiber, 23 g pro.
Daily Values: 116% vit. A, 72% vit. C, 5% calcium, 5% iron

Thai-Style Shrimp Soup FAST

Lemongrass, a signature ingredient in Thai cooking, contributes the lemon scent and flavor to this simple soup. Look for lemongrass in Asian specialty markets or the produce section of larger supermarkets.

Prep: 20 minutes **Cook:** 4 minutes **Makes:** 3 or 4 servings (about 5 cups)

1   14-ounce can chicken broth

1   small zucchini, cut into matchstick-size pieces (about 1½ cups)

1   green onion, bias-cut into 1¼-inch slices

2   tablespoons minced fresh ginger

2   tablespoons minced fresh lemongrass or 1½ teaspoons finely shredded lemon peel

¼   teaspoon crushed red pepper

12   ounces small shrimp, peeled and deveined

1   14-ounce can unsweetened coconut milk

2   tablespoons shredded fresh basil

2   tablespoons toasted shaved coconut

Fresh basil sprigs (optional)

1 In a saucepan bring broth to boiling. Add zucchini, green onion, ginger, lemongrass, and crushed red pepper. Return to boiling; reduce heat. Simmer, uncovered, for 3 minutes, stirring occasionally.

2 Add shrimp. Simmer, uncovered, for 1 to 3 minutes or until the shrimp turn pink. Add the coconut milk. Heat through (do not boil).

3 To serve, ladle into bowls. Top with shredded basil, coconut, and, if desired, basil sprigs.

Nutrition Facts per serving: 445 cal., 37 g total fat (31 g sat. fat), 115 mg chol., 708 mg sodium, 12 g carbo., 4 g fiber, 21 g pro.
Daily Values: 7% vit. A, 18% vit. C, 8% calcium, 25% iron

Paella Soup ♥

Brighten the menu when you serve this colorful, quick version of Spanish paella. Turmeric gives the rice, shrimp, and pork mixture an inviting yellow glow.

Start to finish: 35 minutes **Makes:** 4 servings (about 6½ cups)

½ cup thinly sliced green
   onions
⅓ cup chopped red sweet
   pepper
1 clove garlic, minced
1 teaspoon cooking oil
1 14-ounce can reduced-
   sodium chicken broth
½ cup uncooked long grain
   rice
1 bay leaf
¼ teaspoon salt
⅛ teaspoon ground red
   pepper
⅛ teaspoon ground turmeric
8 ounces cooked pork, cut
   into ¾-inch cubes
8 ounces peeled and
   deveined fresh shrimp
1 cup frozen peas
2 teaspoons snipped fresh
   oregano

1 In a large saucepan cook green onions, sweet pepper, and garlic in hot oil over medium heat for 2 minutes.

2 Stir in broth, rice, bay leaf, salt, red pepper, and turmeric. Heat to boiling; reduce heat. Simmer, covered, for 15 minutes.

3 Stir pork, shrimp, and peas into the broth mixture. Return to boiling; reduce heat. Simmer, covered, for 3 to 5 minutes more or until the shrimp turn pink. Discard bay leaf. Stir in snipped fresh oregano.

Nutrition Facts per serving: 324 cal., 10 g total fat (3 g sat. fat), 139 mg chol., 879 mg sodium, 25 g carbo., 2 g fiber, 31 g pro.
Daily Values: 13% vit. A, 29% vit. C, 3% calcium, 25% iron

Roasted Corn and Crab Soup ♥

This luscious soup can be the star attraction of a light supper. Or try it as an elegant starter at a sit-down dinner; it will serve 12 as a first-course soup.

Start to finish: 1 hour **Makes:** 6 servings (about 8½ cups)

1 16-ounce package frozen whole kernel corn
1 tablespoon cooking oil
2 large onions, chopped (2 cups)
1½ cups seeded and coarsely chopped red sweet peppers (2 medium)
4 14-ounce cans chicken broth (7¼ cups)
½ teaspoon dried thyme, crushed
⅛ to ¼ teaspoon ground red pepper
⅓ cup all-purpose flour
½ cup whipping cream
⅔ cup cooked crabmeat, cut into bite-size pieces, cartilage removed (4 ounces)
Fresh thyme sprigs (optional)

1 Thaw frozen corn and pat dry with paper towels. Line a 15×10×1-inch baking pan with foil; use a little of the cooking oil to lightly grease the pan.

2 Spread corn in prepared pan. Roast, uncovered, in a 450° oven for 10 minutes; stir. Continue to roast about 10 minutes more until golden brown, stirring once or twice. Remove pan from oven; set aside.

3 In a 4-quart Dutch oven cook onions and sweet peppers in remaining oil over medium heat for 3 to 4 minutes or until nearly tender. Add the corn, 3 cans of the broth (about 5½ cups), thyme, and ground red pepper. Bring to boiling; reduce heat. Simmer, uncovered, for 15 minutes.

4 In a screw-top jar combine remaining 1 can chicken broth and the flour; cover and shake until smooth. Add flour mixture to soup. Cook and stir over medium heat until slightly thickened and bubbly. Cook and stir for 1 minute more. Stir whipping cream into soup; heat through.

5 To serve, ladle soup into 6 bowls. Divide crabmeat among bowls. If desired, garnish with fresh thyme sprigs.

Nutrition Facts per serving: 229 cal., 7 g total fat (2 g sat. fat), 26 mg chol., 907 mg sodium, 30 g carbo., 4 g fiber, 14 g pro.
Daily Values: 43% vit. A, 113% vit. C, 7% calcium, 9% iron

To Make Ahead: Prepare soup as directed through Step 3. Cool. Chill in a tightly covered container for up to 2 days. To reheat, transfer soup to a 4-quart Dutch oven. Continue as directed in Steps 4 and 5.

Lemon and Scallop Soup ♥ FAST

If you opt for the long-stemmed enoki mushrooms, toss them into the soup at the last moment because they will toughen if heated. The shiitake mushrooms require a little cooking before serving.

Start to finish: 25 minutes **Makes:** 4 servings (about 7 cups)

12 ounces fresh or frozen bay scallops

5 cups reduced-sodium chicken broth or fish stock

½ cup dry white wine, reduced-sodium chicken broth, or fish stock

3 tablespoons snipped fresh cilantro

2 teaspoons finely shredded lemon peel

¼ teaspoon black pepper

1 pound asparagus spears, trimmed and cut into bite-size pieces

1 cup fresh enoki mushrooms or shiitake mushrooms

½ cup sliced green onions

1 tablespoon lemon juice

1 Thaw scallops, if frozen. Rinse well and drain; set aside.

2 In a large saucepan combine the broth, wine, cilantro, lemon peel, and pepper. Bring to boiling.

3 Add scallops, asparagus, shiitake mushrooms (if using), and green onions. Return to boiling; reduce heat. Simmer, uncovered, for 3 to 5 minutes or until asparagus is tender and scallops are opaque.

4 Remove saucepan from heat. Stir in the enoki mushrooms (if using) and lemon juice. Serve immediately.

Nutrition Facts per serving: 153 cal., 2 g total fat (0 g sat. fat), 28 mg chol., 940 mg sodium, 10 g carbo., 2 g fiber, 20 g pro.
Daily Values: 9% vit. A, 50% vit. C, 3% calcium, 6% iron

Shrimp-Tortilla Soup

If you prefer not to fry the tortilla strips, place the strips on an ungreased baking sheet and bake in a 350° oven about 15 minutes or until crisp, stirring once.

Prep: 20 minutes **Cook:** 25 minutes **Makes:** 4 servings (about 4¼ cups)

5   6-inch corn tortillas
     Cooking oil
2   medium carrots, cut into
        thin, bite-size strips
4   green onions, sliced
3   cloves garlic, minced
2   14-ounce cans reduced-
        sodium chicken broth
¼   cup snipped fresh cilantro
¼   teaspoon black pepper
8   ounces fresh or frozen
        shrimp in shells,
        thawed, peeled, and
        deveined
1   cup chopped fresh
        tomatoes
1   cup shredded Monterey
        Jack cheese or crumbled
        queso fresco (4 ounces)
     Chopped avocado
        (optional)
     Cilantro sprigs (optional)

1 Cut tortillas into ½-inch-wide strips. In a large skillet pour cooking oil to a depth of ¼ inch; heat over medium-high heat. Fry tortilla strips, a few at a time, in hot oil about 1½ minutes or until brown and crisp. Using a slotted spoon, transfer the strips to paper towels to drain thoroughly. Set aside.

2 In a large saucepan or Dutch oven heat 1 tablespoon cooking oil. Cook carrots, green onions, and garlic in hot oil over medium heat for 5 minutes, stirring frequently. Stir in broth, snipped cilantro, and pepper. Bring to boiling; reduce heat. Simmer, covered, for 10 minutes.

3 Meanwhile, place half of the tortilla strips in a blender container or food processor bowl; cover and blend or process until tortilla strips are finely crushed. Stir crushed tortillas into soup; cover and cook for 5 minutes more.

4 Stir in shrimp; cook for 1 to 3 minutes or until shrimp turn pink. Stir in chopped tomatoes. Ladle soup into bowls. Top with cheese and remaining tortilla strips. If desired, garnish with avocado and cilantro sprigs.

Nutrition Facts per serving (with fried tortillas): 311 cal., 14 g total fat (6 g sat. fat), 90 mg chol., 747 mg sodium, 27 g carbo., 3 g fiber, 21 g pro.
Daily Values: 171% vit. A, 33% vit. C, 30% calcium, 21% iron

soup toppers

If you're one who can't resist crushing crackers into your soup, you'll want to add one of these savory toppers to your next bowl.

Garlic Toasts: Toast one side of 1-inch slices of Italian or French bread under the broiler. Turn bread over. Brush with melted butter. Sprinkle with garlic salt and snipped fresh parsley. If desired, sprinkle with grated Parmesan cheese. Broil until toasted. Ladle soup into bowls; float toasts on soup.

Cheese Toasts: Toast bread slices (any kind) under the broiler. Turn and top with shredded cheese. Broil until cheese melts. Ladle soup into bowls; float toasts on soup.

Herbed Croutons: Place 2 cups 1- to 1½-inch cubes French or Italian bread (about 2 ounces) in a bowl. In a large skillet heat 1 tablespoon cooking oil and 1 tablespoon butter over medium-low heat. Add 2 large cloves garlic, minced, and 1 teaspoon dried Italian seasoning, crushed. Cook and stir for 30 seconds. Drizzle over bread cubes, tossing to coat well. Pour cubes into skillet. Cook, stirring occasionally, over medium-low heat for 6 to 8 minutes or until cubes are light brown and crisp. Remove from pan. Drain on paper towels. Store in tightly covered container for up to 1 week.

Cracker Mix: In a large bowl combine 1 cup bite-size fish-shape pretzels or cheese-flavored crackers, 1 cup oyster crackers, 1 cup bite-size shredded wheat biscuits, and 1 cup miniature rich round crackers. In a small bowl combine 2 tablespoons cooking oil, ½ teaspoon Worcestershire sauce, ⅛ teaspoon garlic powder, and dash bottled hot pepper sauce; pour over cracker mixture, tossing to coat. Sprinkle cracker mixture with 2 tablespoons grated Parmesan cheese; toss to coat. Spread mixture on 15×10×1-inch baking pan. Bake in a 300° oven for 10 to 15 minutes or until golden, stirring once. Cool completely. Store in an airtight container for up to 1 week. Sprinkle over soups as desired.

Dumplings for Stew: In a medium bowl combine 1 cup all-purpose flour, 1 teaspoon baking powder, and ½ teaspoon salt. Cut in 2 tablespoons shortening until mixture resembles coarse crumbs. Add ½ cup buttermilk, stirring just until moistened. Thicken stew as directed in recipe. Spoon dumpling batter into mounds on top of stew. Return stew to boiling; reduce heat. Simmer, covered, for 12 to 15 minutes or until a wooden toothpick inserted in dumplings comes out clean. Do not lift cover while simmering.

garnishing ideas

If you're in a rush, here are a few simple ideas to add a finishing touch to bowls of soup:
- Enoki mushrooms
- Fresh herb sprigs or chopped fresh herbs (marjoram, thyme, dill, rosemary, oregano)
- Julienne strips of carrot, leek, fennel, sweet pepper, or green onion
- Thin slices of Parmesan or Romano cheese
- Cheese curls cut from a wedge of cheese with a vegetable peeler

Shrimp and Coconut Soup FAST

This easy-to-make, curry-flavored soup is a favorite in Brazil. Curry was introduced to South America by Portuguese who had once lived on an island off the coast of India.

Start to finish: 15 minutes **Makes:** 5 servings (about 5½ cups)

½ pound fresh or frozen peeled, deveined small shrimp

2 14-ounce cans chicken broth

4 ounces dried angel-hair pasta or vermicelli, broken into 2-inch pieces

1 tablespoon curry powder

1 cup canned unsweetened coconut milk

Sliced green onion or snipped fresh chives

1 Thaw shrimp, if frozen. Rinse shrimp and pat dry. Set aside.

2 In a large saucepan bring broth to boiling. Add pasta and curry powder. Return to boiling. Boil gently for 3 minutes. Add the shrimp; cook for 2 to 3 minutes or until shrimp turn pink and the pasta is tender. Stir in coconut milk; heat through. Ladle soup into bowls; sprinkle with green onion.

Nutrition Facts per serving: 268 cal., 14 g total fat (11 g sat. fat), 69 mg chol., 762 mg sodium, 22 g carbo., 2 g fiber, 15 g pro.
Daily Values: 2% vit. A, 4% vit. C, 4% calcium, 17% iron

Shrimp and Greens Soup ♥ FAST

Although delicious any time of the year, this fresh-tasting soup is light enough to serve during the summer. Lemon-pepper seasoning accents the savory combination of shrimp, bok choy, and leek.

Start to finish: 30 minutes **Makes:** 4 servings (about 7 cups)

12 ounces fresh or frozen peeled, deveined shrimp

1 large leek, sliced

2 cloves garlic, minced

1 tablespoon olive oil

3 14-ounce cans reduced-sodium chicken broth or vegetable broth

1 tablespoon snipped fresh Italian flat-leaf parsley

1 tablespoon snipped fresh marjoram or thyme

¼ teaspoon lemon-pepper seasoning

2 cups shredded bok choy or spinach leaves

1 Thaw shrimp, if frozen. Rinse shrimp; set aside.

2 In a large saucepan cook leek and garlic in hot oil over medium-high heat about 2 minutes or until leek is tender.

3 Carefully add broth, parsley, marjoram, and lemon-pepper seasoning. Bring to boiling; add shrimp. Return to boiling; reduce heat. Simmer, uncovered, for 2 minutes. Stir in the bok choy. Cook about 1 minute more or until the shrimp turn pink.

Nutrition Facts per serving: 147 cal., 6 g total fat (1 g sat. fat), 131 mg chol., 1,093 mg sodium, 5 g carbo., 18 g pro.
Daily Values: 10% vit. A, 25% vit. C, 6% calcium, 18% iron

Sherried Salmon Bisque FAST

You'll love the simplicity of this exquisitely creamy soup. The superb combination of sherry, leeks, salmon, and cream makes this luscious dish worthy of any special occasion.

Start to finish: 25 minutes **Makes:** 2 servings (about 4 cups)

6 ounces fresh or frozen salmon steaks, cut ¾ inch thick
1 tablespoon butter
1½ cups sliced fresh shiitake or other mushrooms
⅓ cup thinly sliced leeks or ¼ cup thinly sliced green onion
1 cup chicken broth or fish stock
¾ teaspoon snipped fresh dill or ¼ teaspoon dried dillweed
Dash black pepper
1 cup half-and-half or light cream
1 tablespoon cornstarch
1 tablespoon dry sherry

1 Thaw the salmon, if frozen. Discard skin and bones. Set salmon aside.

2 Melt butter in a large saucepan over medium heat. Add the mushrooms and leeks; cook for 1 to 2 minutes or until tender. Stir in broth, dried dillweed (if using), and pepper. Bring to boiling.

3 In a small bowl stir together half-and-half and cornstarch. Stir cornstarch mixture into mushroom mixture. Cook and stir over medium heat until thickened and bubbly. Add salmon. Bring to boiling; reduce heat. Simmer, covered, about 4 minutes or until fish flakes easily when tested with a fork. Gently stir in the dry sherry and fresh dill (if using).

Nutrition Facts per serving: 365 cal., 24 g total fat (14 g sat. fat), 75 mg chol., 563 mg sodium, 18 g carbo., 3 g fiber, 20 g pro.
Daily Values: 24% vit. A, 13% calcium, 17% iron

fresh out of fresh

If you're all out of fresh herbs, substitute the dried counterpart. To do so, use one-third the amount of dried herb for the amount of fresh herb called for in a recipe. For example, substitute 1 teaspoon dried herb for 1 tablespoon fresh herb. Before adding a dried herb to a soup, crush it between your fingers and thumb to help release the herb's flavor. Add dried herbs at the beginning of cooking to develop the flavor. If you use a fresh herb, add it at the end because long cooking can destroy its flavor and color. The exception to the rule is fresh rosemary, which can withstand long cooking times.

Spicy Corn Chowder ♥

Corn chowder takes a southwestern detour in this piquant rendition. Using your blender, create your own healthful creamed corn to add creamy richness to this hearty soup.

Prep: 15 minutes **Cook:** 25 minutes **Makes:** 4 servings (about 6 cups)

¼ cup chopped onion
1 clove garlic, minced
½ bulb fennel, chopped
½ medium red sweet pepper, chopped
2 teaspoons olive oil
1 small canned chipotle chile pepper in adobo sauce, chopped
1 to 2 teaspoons adobo sauce
8 ounces red potato, diced (1 cup)
1 14-ounce can reduced-sodium chicken broth
½ cup dry white wine or additional broth
1½ cups fresh or frozen corn kernels
¼ cup water
1 cup fat-free milk
2 tablespoons nonfat dry milk powder
2 teaspoons cornstarch
6 ounces flake- or chunk-style imitation crabmeat, lobster, or scallops
¼ cup snipped fresh cilantro
¼ to ½ teaspoon coarse ground black pepper

1 In a heavy large saucepan cook onion, garlic, fennel, and sweet pepper in hot oil over medium heat about 5 minutes or until tender. Add chipotle pepper, adobo sauce, potato, broth, wine, ½ cup of the corn, and water. Bring to boiling; reduce heat. Simmer, covered, about 10 minutes or until potato is tender.

2 Meanwhile, place remaining 1 cup corn, milk, milk powder, and cornstarch in a blender container; cover and blend until nearly smooth. Add to saucepan; cook and stir until slightly thickened and bubbly; cook and stir 2 minutes more. Stir in imitation seafood, cilantro, and black pepper. Heat through.

Nutrition Facts per serving: 231 cal., 4 g total fat (1 g sat. fat), 14 mg chol., 384 mg sodium, 33 g carbo., 6 g fiber, 14 g pro.
Daily Values: 26% vit. A, 67% vit. C, 14% calcium, 10% iron

To Make Ahead: Prepare soup as directed. Cover and chill for up to 1 day; reheat in a covered saucepan over medium-low heat.

North Sea Chowder ♥ FAST

Try serving this quick, tomato-based chowder with lefse (a very thin Scandinavian potato bread) or crusty French bread.

Prep: 10 minutes **Cook:** 10 minutes **Makes:** 4 to 6 servings (about 8 cups)

1 pound fresh or frozen skinless, boneless sea bass, red snapper, and/or catfish fillets
½ cup chopped onion
2 cloves garlic, minced
1 tablespoon butter
2 fish bouillon cubes
1 tablespoon lemon juice
½ teaspoon instant chicken bouillon granules
½ teaspoon dried thyme, crushed
¼ teaspoon fennel seeds
Dash powdered saffron (optional)
1 bay leaf
4 roma tomatoes, halved lengthwise and thinly sliced

1 Thaw fish, if frozen. Cut into ¾-inch cubes. Set aside.

2 In a large saucepan cook onion and garlic in hot butter over medium heat until tender. Stir in 4 cups water, the fish bouillon cubes, lemon juice, chicken bouillon granules, thyme, fennel, saffron (if using), and bay leaf. Cook and stir until boiling.

3 Add fish and tomatoes. Return to boiling; reduce heat. Simmer, covered, about 10 minutes or until fish flakes easily when tested with a fork. Discard bay leaf. If desired, garnish with fresh thyme sprigs.

Nutrition Facts per serving: 160 cal., 5 g total fat (2 g sat. fat), 55 mg chol., 683 mg sodium, 6 g carbo., 1 g fiber, 22 g pro.
Daily Values: 12% vit. A, 31% vit. C, 2% calcium, 5% iron

quick tomato peeling and seeding

I like to remove the peels and seeds from tomatoes before adding them to soups or stews. Here's an easy way: Cut a shallow X on the bottom of the tomato. Dip it into a pan of boiling water for 15 seconds; rinse with cold water. After the tomato has cooled, use a paring knife to gently pull on the peel where the scored skin has begun to split. The skin will slip off easily. To remove the seeds, cut the tomato in half crosswise. Holding one half over a bowl, use the tip of a spoon to scoop out the seeds.

Maryellyn Krantz
Test Kitchen Home Economist

Red Seafood Chowder

Puff pastry makes an appealing topper for this flavorful soup. When puff pastry toppers don't fit into your schedule, use croutons or crackers instead.

Start to finish: 45 minutes **Makes:** 4 servings (about 6 cups)

½ cup chopped onion
(1 medium)

½ cup chopped fennel (half
of a medium fennel
bulb); reserve leafy tops
for garnish, if desired

1 tablespoon olive oil or
cooking oil

4 medium tomatoes, peeled,
seeded, and cut up

2 14-ounce cans reduced-
sodium chicken broth

¼ teaspoon curry powder

¼ teaspoon black pepper

12 ounces fresh bay scallops
and/or peeled and
deveined medium
shrimp, and/or skinless
fish fillets, such as red
snapper or halibut, cut
into bite-size pieces

½ of a 17¼-ounce package
frozen puff pastry
(1 sheet), thawed
Fennel tops (optional)

1 In a large saucepan cook onion and fennel in hot oil over medium heat until tender. Stir in the tomatoes, broth, curry powder, and pepper. Bring to boiling; reduce heat. Simmer, covered, for 15 minutes.

2 Add scallops, shrimp, and/or fish to saucepan. Return to boiling; reduce heat. Simmer, uncovered, for 2 to 3 minutes more or until scallops and/or shrimp are opaque and fish flakes easily when tested with a fork.

3 Meanwhile, unfold puff pastry onto a floured surface. Cut into 8 squares, triangles, rounds, or other shapes with a sharp knife or cookie cutter. Place on an ungreased baking sheet. Bake in a 400° oven about 10 minutes or until golden and puffed.

4 To serve, ladle hot chowder into bowls. Top each with a piece of baked puff pastry. If desired, garnish with fennel tops.

Nutrition Facts per serving: 431 cal., 24 g total fat (1 g sat. fat), 28 mg chol., 861 mg sodium, 34 g carbo., 5 g fiber, 21 g pro.
Daily Values: 11% vit. A, 58% vit. C, 6% calcium, 9% iron

Salmon Pan Chowder

For extra pepper pep, substitute a dark green poblano pepper and a red jalapeño pepper for the green sweet pepper and red sweet pepper.

Prep: 25 minutes **Cook:** 28 minutes **Makes:** 4 servings (about 4½ cups)

Nonstick cooking spray
1¼ cups white and/or purple
      pearl onions, peeled
1 medium red sweet pepper,
      cut into ½-inch strips
1 medium yellow sweet
      pepper, cut into ½-inch
      strips
1 medium green sweet
      pepper, cut into ½-inch
      strips
1 large banana pepper, cut
      into ¼-inch rings
1 14-ounce can vegetable
      broth or chicken broth
1 cup whipping cream
½ teaspoon caraway seeds,
      lightly crushed
¼ teaspoon salt
4 2-ounce skinless, boneless
      salmon fillets
   Fresh dill sprigs (optional)

1 Lightly coat a Dutch oven with nonstick cooking spray; heat pan. Add onions. Cook and stir over medium-high heat about 7 minutes or until tender. Add sweet peppers and banana pepper. Cook and stir for 1 minute more. Carefully add broth. Bring just to boiling; reduce heat. Simmer, uncovered, for 10 minutes. Stir in whipping cream. Return to boiling; reduce heat. Simmer for 10 minutes.

2 Meanwhile, rub caraway seeds and salt on both sides of fish. Coat a medium skillet with cooking spray; heat skillet. Cook fillets, uncovered, over medium-high heat for 3 to 4 minutes per side or until fish flakes easily when tested with a fork.

3 To serve, place a salmon fillet in each of four shallow bowls. Ladle soup mixture over salmon fillets. If desired, top with fresh dill sprigs.

Nutrition Facts per serving: 327 cal., 25 g total fat (14 g sat. fat), 112 mg chol., 647 mg sodium, 14 g carbo., 3 g fiber, 15 g pro.
Daily Values: 48% vit. A, 233% vit. C, 11% calcium, 6% iron

Maryland Crab and Corn Chowder

In Maryland, rich and creamy chowders such as this one are traditionally made with blue crabs from Chesapeake Bay. Any type of crabmeat will be equally delicious in this rich and savory soup.

Start to finish: 40 minutes **Makes:** 6 servings (about 4½ cups)

6 ounces fresh or frozen cooked crabmeat

1½ cups frozen whole kernel corn

1 medium onion, finely chopped (½ cup)

2 cloves garlic, minced

1 teaspoon cooking oil

1 14-ounce can chicken broth

1 cup whipping cream

⅛ teaspoon ground white pepper

1 medium potato, peeled and finely chopped (1 cup)

¼ cup finely chopped red, yellow, or green sweet pepper

Snipped fresh parsley (optional)

Red sweet pepper strips (optional)

1 Thaw crabmeat, if frozen. In a 2-quart saucepan cook half of the corn, the onion, and garlic in hot oil over medium heat until onion is tender. Carefully add broth. Bring to boiling; reduce heat. Simmer, uncovered, for 10 minutes. Stir in cream and white pepper. Simmer, uncovered, about 10 minutes more or until slightly thickened. Cool slightly.

2 Place cream mixture in a blender container or food processor bowl. Cover and blend or process until smooth. Return cream mixture to saucepan. Keep warm.

3 Meanwhile, in a small saucepan cook the remaining corn and the potato in boiling, salted water 5 minutes. Add chopped sweet pepper. Cook 1 minute more. Drain; stir into cream mixture in saucepan. Add crab; heat through. If desired, garnish each serving with parsley and red sweet pepper strips.

Nutrition Facts per serving: 249 cal., 17 g total fat (10 g sat. fat), 83 mg chol., 308 mg sodium, 16 g carbo., 2 g fiber, 10 g pro.
Daily Values: 19% vit. A, 36% vit. C, 7% calcium, 5% iron

Effortless Shrimp Chowder ♥ FAST

Enjoy this fast-fix chowder with toasted sesame or rye crackers as a quick and easy lunch. Or turn your creamy chowder into heartier fare by serving it with hot garlic bread and a crisp green salad.

Start to finish: 10 minutes **Makes:** 4 servings (about 3½ cups)

1 10¾-ounce can condensed cream of shrimp soup
1 cup milk, half-and-half, or light cream
¼ cup cream sherry, dry sherry, or milk
1 tablespoon butter (optional)
8 ounces fresh or frozen small shrimp, peeled and deveined (about 1 cup)
   Cilantro sprigs (optional)

1 In a 2-quart saucepan combine soup, milk, and sherry. Bring just to boiling. If desired, add butter. Reduce heat. Simmer, uncovered, for 5 minutes, stirring often.

2 If desired, chop shrimp. Add shrimp to soup mixture. Return to boiling; reduce heat. Simmer for 1 to 2 minutes more or until shrimp turn pink. To serve, ladle into bowls. If desired, garnish with cilantro sprigs.

Nutrition Facts per serving: 138 cal., 5 g total fat (2 g sat. fat), 80 mg chol., 699 mg sodium, 9 g carbo., 0 g fiber, 11 g pro.
Daily Values: 8% calcium, 9% iron

Salmon Confetti Chowder ♥ FAST

Frozen stir-fry vegetables, refrigerated packaged potatoes, and canned salmon guarantee off-the-shelf convenience. Fat-free half-and-half and fat-free milk keep the calories in check.

Prep: 15 minutes **Cook:** 12 minutes **Makes:** 4 servings (about 7 cups)

2 cups frozen stir-fry vegetables (yellow, green, and red pepper and onion)

2 tablespoons minced, seeded jalapeño pepper (see tip, page 12)

1 tablespoon butter

2 tablespoons all-purpose flour

2 cups fat-free milk

1 cup fat-free half-and-half

2 cups refrigerated diced potatoes with onions

1 15-ounce can salmon, drained and flaked

¼ cup snipped watercress

2 tablespoons lemon juice

½ teaspoon salt

½ teaspoon black pepper

1 In a large saucepan cook the stir-fry vegetables and jalapeño pepper in hot butter over medium heat for 3 to 5 minutes or until tender. Stir in flour. Stir in milk and half-and-half. Cook and stir until slightly thickened. Cook and stir for 2 minutes more.

2 Stir in potatoes, salmon, watercress, lemon juice, salt, and black pepper. Cook and stir until heated through.

Nutrition Facts per serving: 349 cal., 10 g total fat (3 g sat. fat), 69 mg chol., 1,174 mg sodium, 33 g carbo., 3 g fiber, 29 g pro.
Daily Values: 11% vit. A, 25% vit. C, 42% calcium, 8% iron

Creamy Shrimp and Spinach Stew FAST

A dash of nutmeg brings out the best in shrimp and emphasizes the slightly sweet, nutty taste of the Gruyère cheese. Be sure to use process cheese for a velvety smooth soup.

Start to finish: 30 minutes **Makes:** 4 servings (about 4 cups)

8 ounces fresh or frozen, peeled, deveined small shrimp
1 cup sliced fresh button, shiitake, and/or cremini mushrooms
1 medium onion, chopped (½ cup)
1 clove garlic, minced
2 tablespoons butter
3 tablespoons all-purpose flour
1 bay leaf
⅛ teaspoon ground nutmeg
⅛ teaspoon black pepper
1 14-ounce can vegetable or chicken broth
1 cup half-and-half, light cream, or milk
¾ cup shredded process Gruyère cheese (3 ounces)
2 cups torn fresh spinach

1 Thaw shrimp, if frozen. Rinse shrimp; set aside.

2 In a medium saucepan cook mushrooms, onion, and garlic in hot butter over medium heat until tender. Stir in flour, bay leaf, nutmeg, and pepper. Add broth and half-and-half all at once. Cook and stir until mixture is thickened and bubbly.

3 Add shrimp. Cook for 2 minutes more. Add Gruyère cheese and stir until cheese melts. Discard bay leaf. Stir in spinach. Serve immediately.

Nutrition Facts per serving: 326 cal., 22 g total fat (12 g sat. fat), 148 mg chol., 676 mg sodium, 11 g carbo., 2 g fiber, 23 g pro.
Daily Values: 36% vit. A, 11% vit. C, 33% calcium, 17% iron

Caribbean Seafood Stew

Coconut milk softens the burn of the jalapeño pepper in this fish and shrimp stew. Those who like more heat can add bottled hot pepper sauce at the table.

Start to finish: 45 minutes **Makes:** 4 to 6 servings (about 5 cups)

1 pound fresh or frozen skinless red snapper, cod, or haddock fillets

8 ounces fresh or frozen peeled, deveined medium shrimp

2 tablespoons olive oil

1 tablespoon lime juice

¼ teaspoon salt

⅛ teaspoon black pepper

1 large onion, chopped (1 cup)

1 cup chopped green sweet pepper

6 cloves garlic, minced (1 tablespoon)

1 jalapeño pepper, seeded and finely chopped (see tip, page 12)

1 14½-ounce can diced tomatoes, undrained

½ cup canned unsweetened coconut milk

½ cup snipped fresh cilantro

2 cups hot cooked rice

2 tablespoons snipped fresh cilantro

Bottled hot pepper sauce (optional)

1 Thaw fish and shrimp, if frozen. Rinse well. Cut fish into 1-inch cubes.

2 In a medium bowl stir together 1 tablespoon of the olive oil, lime juice, salt, and black pepper. Add fish cubes; toss to coat. Set aside.

3 In a 3-quart saucepan heat remaining oil over medium-high heat. Add the onion, sweet pepper, garlic, and jalapeño pepper. Cook and stir about 4 minutes or until the onion is tender. Stir in undrained tomatoes and coconut milk. Bring to boiling; reduce heat. Simmer, uncovered, for 10 minutes, stirring occasionally.

4 Stir in shrimp, fish mixture, and the ½ cup cilantro. Return to boiling; reduce heat. Simmer, uncovered, 5 minutes or until fish flakes easily when tested with a fork and shrimp turn pink, stirring occasionally. Serve with hot cooked rice. Sprinkle with the 2 tablespoons cilantro. If desired, pass hot pepper sauce.

Nutrition Facts per serving: 414 cal., 15 g total fat (6 g sat. fat), 147 mg chol., 576 mg sodium, 35 g carbo., 2 g fiber, 35 g pro.
Daily Values: 13% vit. A, 74% vit. C, 7% calcium, 26% iron

Carolina Catfish Stew ♥

With its firm flesh and mild flavor, catfish is a great choice for soups and stews. Bake a pan of corn bread to accompany this Southern-style stew.

Prep: 10 minutes **Cook:** 45 minutes **Makes:** 6 servings (about 9 cups)

1 pound fresh or frozen catfish
2 slices bacon (optional)
1 medium onion, chopped (½ cup)
2 14½-ounce cans stewed tomatoes, undrained
1 8-ounce can tomato sauce
1 cup water
¾ cup dry white wine
2 bay leaves
½ teaspoon black pepper
¼ teaspoon dried thyme, crushed
1 16-ounce can sliced potatoes, drained
1 10-ounce package frozen cut okra

1 Thaw fish, if frozen. Cut fish into bite-size pieces; set aside.

2 In a Dutch oven cook the bacon until crisp; drain on paper towels, reserving bacon drippings in pan. Crumble bacon, set aside. Cook the onion in bacon drippings over medium heat until tender. (If not using bacon, cook the onion in 1 tablespoon hot cooking oil.)

3 Stir in undrained tomatoes, tomato sauce, water, wine, bay leaves, pepper, and thyme. Bring to boiling; reduce heat. Simmer, covered, for 25 minutes.

4 Add the potatoes and okra. Return to boiling; reduce heat. Simmer, covered, for 5 to 10 minutes more or until the okra is almost tender. Add fish; cook about 5 minutes more or until fish flakes easily when tested with a fork. Discard bay leaves. Ladle stew into bowls. If desired, top with the crumbled bacon.

Nutrition Facts per serving: 243 cal., 7 g total fat (1 g sat. fat), 35 mg chol., 702 mg sodium, 25 g carbo., 5 g fiber, 15 g pro.
Daily Values: 10% vit. A, 22% vit. C, 12% calcium, 12% iron

Pearl-of-an-Oyster Stew

In this easy variation on the traditional oyster stew, mellow leeks complement the delicate flavor of the oysters. If you like, substitute two additional cups of half-and-half or light cream for the milk.

Start to finish: 35 minutes **Makes:** 8 servings (about 9 cups)

⅔ cup sliced leeks
    (2 medium)
2 tablespoons butter
3 tablespoons all-purpose
    flour
1 teaspoon anchovy paste
2 cups half-and-half or light
    cream
2 cups milk
6 cups shucked oysters
    (3 pints)
    Several dashes bottled hot
    pepper sauce (optional)

1 In a 4-quart saucepan cook leeks in hot butter until tender. Stir in flour and anchovy paste until combined. Add half-and-half and milk. Cook and stir until slightly thickened and bubbly. Cook and stir for 1 minute more.

2 Meanwhile, drain the oysters, reserving 3 cups liquid. Strain the liquid.

3 In a large saucepan combine reserved oyster liquid and oysters. Bring just to simmering over medium heat; reduce heat. Cook, covered, about 1 to 2 minutes or until oysters curl around the edges. Skim surface of cooking liquid. Stir oyster mixture into leek mixture. If desired, add hot pepper sauce.

Nutrition Facts per serving: 242 cal., 14 g total fat (9 g sat. fat), 105 mg chol., 248 mg sodium, 15 g carbo., 1 g fiber, 14 g pro.
Daily Values: 27% vit. A, 14% vit. C, 17% calcium, 61% iron

Spicy Mexican-Style Fish Stew ♥ FAST

This full-bodied stew owes its spiciness to crushed red pepper and a can of Mexican-style stewed tomatoes. A mixture of parsley and lemon peel makes a colorful and flavorful topper.

Prep: 15 minutes **Cook:** 10 minutes **Makes:** 4 servings (about 8 cups)

1 pound fresh or frozen
    white fish fillets (such
    as cod or haddock)
2 cups chicken broth, fish
    stock, or vegetable broth
1 cup sliced fresh
    mushrooms
1 cup sliced zucchini or
    yellow summer squash
1 medium onion, chopped
    (½ cup)
1 clove garlic, minced
⅛ teaspoon salt
⅛ teaspoon crushed red
    pepper
1 bay leaf
2 14½-ounce cans Mexican-
    style stewed tomatoes,
    undrained
2 tablespoons snipped fresh
    parsley
½ teaspoon finely shredded
    lemon peel

1 Thaw fish, if frozen. Cut fish into 1-inch pieces; set aside. In a large saucepan or Dutch oven combine broth, mushrooms, zucchini, onion, garlic, salt, crushed red pepper, and bay leaf. Bring to boiling; reduce heat. Simmer, covered, for 5 minutes.

2 Stir in undrained tomatoes and fish. Bring to boiling; reduce heat. Simmer, covered, about 5 minutes more or just until fish flakes easily when tested with a fork. Discard bay leaf.

3 In a small bowl combine parsley and lemon peel. Ladle soup into bowls. Sprinkle with parsley mixture.

Nutrition Facts per serving: 194 cal., 2 g total fat (0 g sat. fat), 49 mg chol., 1,216 mg sodium, 18 g carbo., 1 g fiber, 26 g pro.
Daily Values: 5% vit. A, 66% vit. C, 6% calcium, 9% iron

Moroccan Bouillabaisse

This version of bouillabaisse features the shrimp, scallops, and mussels typical of the classic French stew, but Moroccan spices—cumin, cinnamon, and ground red pepper—replace the classic herbs.

Prep: 1 hour **Cook:** 11 minutes **Makes:** 4 servings (about 5 cups)

8 ounces fresh or frozen shrimp, peeled and deveined
8 ounces fresh or frozen scallops
8 ounces fresh mussels in shells (about 12)
1 cup chopped onion
4 cloves garlic, minced
1 tablespoon olive oil
1 teaspoon ground cumin
½ teaspoon ground cinnamon
¼ teaspoon ground red pepper
1 cup fish or vegetable broth
1 cup finely chopped tomatoes
⅛ teaspoon ground saffron
¼ teaspoon salt
Hot cooked couscous

1 Thaw shrimp and scallops, if frozen. Halve any large scallops. Scrub the mussels with a stiff brush under cold running water. Using your fingers, pull out the beards that are visible between the shells. In a large Dutch oven combine 4 cups water and 3 tablespoons salt; add mussels and soak 15 minutes. Drain; rinse. Repeat soaking mussels two more times.

2 In a large saucepan cook onion and garlic in hot oil over medium heat until tender. Add cumin, cinnamon, and red pepper; cook and stir for 1 minute.

3 Carefully stir in broth, tomatoes, saffron, and salt. Bring to boiling; add scallops and mussels. Return to boiling; reduce heat. Simmer, covered, about 5 minutes or until mussel shells open. Add shrimp; cook, covered, 1 to 2 minutes more or until shrimp turn pink. Serve with couscous.

Nutrition Facts per serving: 273 cal., 6 g total fat (1 g sat. fat), 90 mg chol., 460 mg sodium, 28 g carbo., 3 g fiber, 26 g pro.
Daily Values: 9% vit. A, 27% vit. C, 7% calcium, 16% iron

the lowdown on shrimp

When buying fresh shrimp for recipes, purchase 1½ pounds of raw shrimp in the shell for each pound of shelled shrimp you need. The price of shrimp per pound depends on the size—the bigger the shrimp, the higher the price per pound.

To peel shrimp, start at the head end and use your fingers to peel back the shell. Gently pull on the tail portion of the shell and remove it. To devein a shrimp, use a sharp knife to make a shallow slit along its back from head to tail. Rinse under cold running water to remove the vein, using the tip of a knife to dislodge it, if necessary.

Country Fish Stew ♥

For this home-style stew, use a mild-tasting fish such as cod, haddock, or tilapia. To reduce your prep time, substitute 3 cups packaged coleslaw mix for the shredded cabbage.

Prep: 15 minutes **Cook:** 25 minutes **Makes:** 4 servings (about 7 cups)

1 pound fresh or frozen fish fillets
1 stalk celery, chopped (½ cup)
1 small onion, chopped (⅓ cup)
1 clove garlic, minced
2 tablespoons butter
3 cups Fish Stock (see recipe, page 88), vegetable broth, or chicken broth
½ small head cabbage, coarsely chopped (about 3 cups)
¼ cup chopped bottled roasted red sweet pepper
½ teaspoon lemon-pepper seasoning
1 15-ounce can Great Northern beans, rinsed and drained
2 tablespoons snipped fresh parsley

1 Thaw fish, if frozen. Rinse fish; pat dry with paper towels. Cut fish into 1-inch pieces; set aside.

2 In a large saucepan cook celery, onion, and garlic in hot butter over medium-high heat for 4 to 5 minutes or until tender but not brown, stirring often.

3 Add the stock, cabbage, red pepper, and lemon-pepper seasoning. Bring to boiling; reduce heat. Simmer, covered, for 15 minutes, stirring occasionally.

4 Add beans and fish. Return to boiling; reduce heat. Simmer, covered, about 5 minutes or until fish flakes easily when tested with a fork, stirring once. Ladle stew into bowls. Sprinkle with snipped parsley.

Nutrition Facts per serving: 299 cal., 9 g total fat (4 g sat. fat), 72 mg chol., 836 mg sodium, 21 g carbo., 7 g fiber, 32 g pro.
Daily Values: 9% vit. A, 80% vit. C, 15% calcium, 15% iron

Meatless

Greek Minestrone

In This Chapter:

A to Z Vegetable Soup 126
Bean and Brussels
    Sprouts Stew 155
Caramelized Onion Soup 132
Cheesy Cauliflower
    Chowder 147
Chunky Ratatouille Stew 156
Corn and Cheese
    Chowder 148
Emerald Soup 141
Garbanzo Bean Stew 152
Greek Minestrone 131
Herb and Pepper
    Lentil Stew 153
Hot-and-Sour Tofu Soup 134

Italian Bean Soup 122
Italian Lentil Soup 128
Lentil-Spinach Soup 143
Mushroom and Tofu Soup 130
Potato-Beet Soup 142
Potato-Curry Soup 138
Roasted Garlic-Potato
    Soup 125
Root Vegetable and
    Bean Soup 137
Split Pea Soup with
    Spiced Yogurt 146
Spring Vegetable Soup 139
Springtime Soup 121
Squash Soup with Ravioli 123

Thai Peanut Soup 124
Tortellini and
    Vegetable Soup 136
Two-Bean Chili 150
Vegetable Broth 120
Vegetable Chili
    with Cheese 149
Veggie Soup with
    Curry Croutons 145
White Bean and
    Cumin Chili 151
Wild Rice and
    Cheese Soup 129
Winter Vegetable Soup 135

Vegetable Broth ♥

Favorite soup veggies—onions, carrots, parsnips, and cabbage—combine to make this full-of-flavor vegetarian broth. Use it in any recipe that calls for vegetable broth or stock.

Prep: 30 minutes **Cook:** 2 hours **Makes:** about 7 cups

4 medium yellow onions, unpeeled
4 medium carrots
3 medium potatoes
2 medium parsnips, turnips, or rutabagas
1 small head cabbage
1 tablespoon olive oil
8 cups water
1 teaspoon salt
½ teaspoon dried dillweed, basil, rosemary, or marjoram, crushed
¼ teaspoon black pepper

1 Scrub all vegetables; cut off root and stem ends. Do not peel vegetables unless coated with wax. Cut onions into wedges. Cut carrots, potatoes, parsnips, and cabbage into 2-inch pieces.

2 In a 6-quart kettle or Dutch oven heat oil over medium heat. Add vegetables. Cook and stir about 10 minutes or until vegetables start to brown. Stir in water, salt, dillweed, and pepper. Bring to boiling; reduce heat. Simmer, covered, for 2 hours.

3 Strain stock (see page 5). Discard vegetable mixture. Place stock in a storage container. Cover and chill for up to 3 days or freeze for up to 6 months.

Nutrition Facts per 1 cup: 17 cal., 2 g total fat (0 g sat. fat), 313 mg sodium

sodium comparisons

If the wonderful flavor of homemade broth and stock isn't enough of a temptation to get out a stockpot, take a look at the sodium content of canned broths. If you're concerned about sodium in your diet, homemade is best. This is especially true if you're using vegetable broth, which is not readily available in a reduced-sodium form.

1 cup canned chicken broth	776 mg
1 cup canned reduced-sodium chicken broth	620 mg
1 cup canned beef broth	820 mg
1 cup reduced-sodium beef broth	440 mg
1 cup canned vegetable broth	1,000 mg

Springtime Soup ♥ FAST

Garden-fresh asparagus, snow peas, and spinach make this quick-to-fix tempter a vegetarian treat. If you enjoy the fragrance and flavor of basil, be sure to include the pesto.

Start to finish: 25 minutes **Makes:** 8 servings (about 12 cups)

1 pound fresh asparagus spears
1 medium onion, chopped (½ cup)
3 cloves garlic, minced
1 tablespoon olive oil
6 cups vegetable broth
½ cup dried orzo or other small pasta
3 cups snow pea pods, ends and strings removed
6 cups torn fresh spinach
¼ teaspoon black pepper
¼ cup purchased or homemade pesto (optional)
¼ cup finely shredded Parmesan cheese (1 ounce)

1 Snap off and discard woody bases from asparagus. If desired, scrape off scales. Bias-slice the asparagus into 1-inch pieces; set aside.

2 Meanwhile, in a 4-quart Dutch oven cook the onion and garlic in hot oil over medium heat until tender. Carefully add broth; bring to boiling. Stir in pasta; reduce heat and boil gently for 5 minutes. Stir in asparagus and snow pea pods. Return to boiling; cook for 3 minutes more. Stir in spinach and pepper; cook for 1 minute more. Remove soup from heat.

3 Ladle soup into bowls. If desired, swirl 1 to 2 teaspoons pesto into each bowl of soup. Sprinkle with Parmesan cheese.

Nutrition Facts per serving: 133 cal., 4 g total fat (1 g sat. fat), 3 mg chol., 802 mg sodium, 15 g carbo., 3 g fiber, 10 g pro.
Daily Values: 31% vit. A, 59% vit. C, 8% calcium, 18% iron

Italian Bean Soup ♥

Float thick slices of buttered garlic toast on this hearty meat-free soup. Three kinds of beans—Great Northern, red beans, and Italian-style green beans—provide plenty of protein and vitamins.

Prep: 20 minutes **Stand:** 1 hour **Cook:** 10½ to 12½ hours **Makes:** 6 servings (about 10 cups)

1   cup dry Great Northern beans
1   cup dry red beans or pinto beans
5   cups cold water
3   14-ounce cans vegetable broth
1   medium onion, chopped (½ cup)
2   cloves garlic, minced
2   teaspoons dried Italian seasoning, crushed
¼   teaspoon black pepper
1   14½-ounce can diced tomatoes with basil, oregano, and garlic, undrained
1   9-ounce package frozen Italian green beans or cut green beans
2   tablespoons balsamic vinegar
2   tablespoons butter, softened
¼   teaspoon garlic powder
¼   teaspoon dried Italian seasoning, crushed
12 ½-inch slices baguette-style French bread

1 Rinse beans. In a Dutch oven combine beans and cold water. Bring to boiling; reduce heat. Simmer, uncovered, for 10 minutes. Remove from heat. Cover and let stand for 1 hour. Drain and rinse beans.

2 In a 4- to 5-quart slow cooker combine the beans, broth, onion, garlic, the 2 teaspoons Italian seasoning, and black pepper.

3 Cover and cook on low-heat setting for 10 to 12 hours or on high-heat setting for 5 to 6 hours or until the beans are almost tender.

4 If using low-heat setting, turn to high-heat setting. Stir undrained tomatoes and frozen green beans into bean mixture. Cover and cook on high-heat setting about 30 minutes more or until beans are tender. Stir in balsamic vinegar.

5 Meanwhile, in a small bowl stir together butter, garlic powder, and the ¼ teaspoon Italian seasoning. Spread on 1 side of each bread slice. Place bread on the unheated rack of a broiler pan or on a baking sheet. Broil 4 to 5 inches from the heat for 1 to 2 minutes or until crisp and light brown. To serve, ladle soup into bowls. Add 2 pieces of herb toast to each bowl of soup. Serve immediately.

Nutrition Facts per serving: 384 cal., 6 g total fat (3 g sat. fat), 11 mg chol., 1,384 mg sodium, 66 g carbo., 14 g fiber, 20 g pro.
Daily Values: 18% vit. A, 21% vit. C, 16% calcium, 28% iron

Squash Soup with Ravioli ♥

When halving the squash, use a carving or chef's knife that's longer than the squash. Push the knife down with the palm of your hand and use a rocking motion to cut through the hard shell.

Start to finish: 50 minutes **Makes:** 5 servings (about 6½ cups)

2	pounds butternut squash
2	14-ounce cans vegetable broth
½	cup water
⅛	teaspoon ground red pepper
1	tablespoon butter
1	9-ounce package refrigerated cheese ravioli
1	tablespoon molasses

1 Peel squash. Halve lengthwise. Remove seeds and discard. Cut squash into ¾-inch pieces.

2 In a large saucepan combine squash, broth, water, and ground red pepper. Bring to boiling; reduce heat. Simmer, covered, about 20 minutes or until squash is tender.

3 Place one-fourth of the squash mixture in a blender container or food processor bowl. Cover and blend or process until smooth. Repeat 3 more times with the remaining mixture. Return all of the mixture to the saucepan. Bring to boiling; reduce heat. Simmer, uncovered, for 5 minutes. Add butter, stirring until melted.

4 Meanwhile, cook the ravioli according to package directions. Drain. Ladle hot soup into bowls. Divide cooked ravioli among bowls. Drizzle with molasses.

Nutrition Facts per serving: 259 cal., 10 g total fat (6 g sat. fat), 57 mg chol., 933 mg sodium, 36 g carbo., 2 g fiber, 10 g pro.
Daily Values: 95% vit. A, 40% vit. C, 18% calcium, 10% iron

To Make Ahead: Prepare soup as directed, except do not add ravioli. Cool soup. Transfer to an airtight container. Store in the refrigerator up to 2 days or label and freeze for up to 3 months. To reheat, transfer frozen soup to a large saucepan. Cook, covered, over medium-low heat for 15 to 20 minutes or until heated through, stirring often. Continue as directed in Step 4.

Thai Peanut Soup FAST

This creamy soup blends flavors popular in Thai recipes, including peanuts, coconut, and lemongrass. A bit of ground red pepper adds heat. Balance these pungent flavors with a crisp green salad.

Start to finish: 30 minutes **Makes:** 4 servings (about 4 cups)

⅓ cup finely chopped onion
⅓ cup finely chopped celery
½ cup finely chopped red
    sweet pepper
1 tablespoon butter
1 tablespoon all-purpose
    flour
1 tablespoon very finely
    chopped lemongrass
    (white portion only) or
    1 teaspoon finely
    shredded lemon peel
¼ teaspoon ground red
    pepper
1 14-ounce can vegetable
    broth
1 13½-ounce can
    unsweetened coconut
    milk
¼ cup creamy peanut butter
1 tablespoon soy sauce
    Chopped peanuts
    (optional)
    Snipped fresh cilantro
    (optional)

1 In a 2-quart saucepan cook onion, celery, and ¼ cup of the red sweet pepper in hot butter over medium heat about 5 minutes or until vegetables are tender, stirring occasionally. Stir in the flour, lemongrass, and ground red pepper. Add broth and coconut milk all at once. Cook and stir until the mixture is slightly thickened and bubbly. Cook and stir for 1 minute more. (Mixture may look curdled.)

2 Stir peanut butter and soy sauce into mixture in saucepan; cook and stir until well mixed and heated through. To serve, ladle soup into bowls. Top with remaining chopped red sweet pepper and, if desired, peanuts and cilantro.

Nutrition Facts per serving: 327 cal., 29 g total fat (20 g sat. fat), 8 mg chol., 780 mg sodium, 12 g carbo., 2 g fiber, 7 g pro.
Daily Values: 26% vit. A, 52% vit. C, 2% calcium, 8% iron

Roasted Garlic-Potato Soup ♥

The potatoes and garlic are roasted before they're added to the soup. Roasting enriches the potatoes' flavor and mellows the garlic.

Prep: 15 minutes **Bake:** 45 minutes **Cook:** 30 minutes **Makes:** 6 servings (about 6 cups)

6 medium baking potatoes (about 2 pounds), peeled and cut into 1-inch pieces
2 tablespoons olive oil
½ teaspoon black pepper
6 cloves garlic, peeled
1 medium onion, chopped (½ cup)
3 cups vegetable broth
1 cup water
1 cup whole milk
1 cup thinly sliced Colby, cheddar, or desired cheese (4 ounces)

1 Place potatoes in a shallow roasting pan. Drizzle with 1 tablespoon of the olive oil. Sprinkle with pepper. Stir to coat.

2 Roast potatoes in a 425° oven, uncovered, for 25 minutes. Turn potatoes with a metal spatula. Add garlic cloves. Roast about 20 minutes more or until potatoes are brown. Set aside 1 cup of the roasted potatoes.

3 In a 3-quart saucepan heat remaining oil. Cook and stir onion over medium-high heat for 5 minutes. Add remaining roasted potatoes and the garlic to onions in saucepan. Stir in broth and water. Bring to boiling; reduce heat. Simmer, covered, about 20 minutes or until potatoes are very tender.

4 Place about half of the potato mixture in a blender container or food processor bowl. Cover and blend or process until nearly smooth. Repeat with remaining mixture. Return all of the mixture to saucepan. Stir in milk. Season to taste with salt. Heat through.

5 To serve, ladle soup into bowls. Top each serving with some of the reserved roasted potatoes and sliced cheese.

Nutrition Facts per serving: 266 cal., 12 g total fat (5 g sat. fat), 23 mg chol., 561 mg sodium, 28 g carbo., 3 g fiber, 11 g pro.
Daily Values: 6% vit. A, 38% vit. C, 20% calcium, 8% iron

A to Z Vegetable Soup ♥

Thin slices of Parmesan cheese make a scrumptious garnish for this colorful soup featuring a medley of garden vegetables. The hot soup softens the cheese to a delightful consistency.

Start to finish: 45 minutes **Makes:** 4 servings (about 5 cups)

1 tablespoon cooking oil or
  olive oil
2 cups cut-up mixed fresh
  vegetables, such as
  sliced small zucchini,
  carrots, or celery, and
  chopped red onions
2 14-ounce cans vegetable
  broth
2 cloves garlic, minced
1 15-ounce can white kidney
  (cannellini) beans or
  Great Northern beans,
  rinsed and drained
½ cup dried alphabet-shaped
  pasta or tiny shells
1 tablespoon snipped fresh
  oregano or 1 teaspoon
  dried oregano, crushed
1 ounce Parmesan cheese,
  thinly sliced (optional)

1 In a large saucepan heat oil over medium heat. Add mixed vegetables. Cook, uncovered, about 5 minutes or until vegetables are crisp-tender, stirring occasionally.

2 Stir broth and garlic into saucepan. Bring to boiling. Stir in beans, pasta, and dried oregano (if using). Return to boiling; reduce heat. Simmer, covered, about 10 minutes or just until pasta is tender. Stir in fresh oregano (if using).

3 To serve, ladle soup into bowls. If desired, top each serving with Parmesan cheese slices.

Nutrition Facts per serving: 166 cal., 5 g total fat (1 g sat. fat), 0 mg chol., 995 mg sodium, 29 g carbo., 6 g fiber, 10 g pro.
Daily Values: 7% vit. A, 8% vit. C, 4% calcium, 11% iron

Italian Lentil Soup ♥

In Italy, lentils are served on New Year's Day as a symbol of wealth and prosperity. Whether or not they bring you wealth, you can count on lentils to provide protein, fiber, vitamins, and minerals.

Prep: 15 minutes **Cook:** 50 minutes **Makes:** 5 servings (about 10 cups)

  2 medium carrots, sliced
       (1 cup)
  1 stalk celery, sliced (½ cup)
  1 small onion, chopped
       (⅓ cup)
  1 tablespoon olive oil
  5 cups water
  ½ of a small head cabbage,
       cored and cut into
       1-inch pieces (4 cups)
  1 cup dried lentils, rinsed
       and drained
  1 cup tomato puree
1½ teaspoons sugar
1½ teaspoons salt
  ½ teaspoon dried oregano,
       crushed
  ¼ teaspoon black pepper

1 In a large saucepan cook carrots, celery, and onion in hot oil over medium heat about 5 minutes or until crisp-tender.

2 Stir in water, cabbage, lentils, tomato puree, sugar, salt, oregano, and pepper. Bring to boiling; reduce heat. Simmer, covered, about 45 minutes or until lentils are very soft.

Nutrition Facts per serving: 210 cal., 3 g total fat (0 g sat. fat), 0 mg chol., 938 mg sodium, 35 g carbo., 15 g fiber, 13 g pro.
Daily Values: 76% vit. A, 49% vit. C, 8% calcium, 26% iron

Wild Rice and Cheese Soup

The heartier flavors of smoked cheese and ale are balanced by the sweetness of chopped apples and the nutty taste of wild rice.

Prep: 40 minutes **Cook:** 12 minutes **Makes:** 4 servings (about 5 cups)

2 cups shredded smoked Gouda or cheddar cheese (8 ounces)

4 teaspoons all-purpose flour

2 teaspoons butter

2 tablespoons finely chopped onion

1 medium cooking apple, cored and chopped (1 cup)

½ cup cooked wild rice

1¼ cups vegetable broth

½ cup brown ale, amber beer, or nonalcoholic beer

¼ teaspoon ground white pepper

⅔ cup half-and-half or light cream

Fresh thyme sprigs (optional)

1 In a bowl toss cheese with flour; set aside.

2 In a 2-quart saucepan melt butter. Add onion; cook and stir about 4 minutes or until tender. Add ¾ of the apple, the cooked rice, broth, beer, and pepper. Bring to boiling; reduce heat. Simmer, uncovered, for 10 minutes.

3 Slowly stir cheese mixture into broth mixture until melted. Stir in half-and-half. Cook just until heated through; do not boil. To serve, ladle into bowls; top with remaining chopped apple. If desired, garnish with fresh thyme sprigs.

Nutrition Facts per serving: 310 cal., 21 g total fat (14 g sat. fat), 66 mg chol., 1,231 mg sodium, 18 g carbo., 1 g fiber, 13 g pro.
Daily Values: 7% vit. A, 4% vit. C, 40% calcium, 2% iron

Mushroom and Tofu Soup ♥ FAST

Japanese udon (oo-DOHN) noodles are similar to spaghetti. Look for them in Asian markets or in the Oriental section of your supermarket.

Start to finish: 30 minutes **Makes:** 6 servings (about 9 cups)

6 cups vegetable broth
1 10- to 12-ounce package extra-firm tofu (fresh bean curd), drained and cut into ½-inch cubes
1 tablespoon soy sauce
1 tablespoon toasted sesame oil
6 ounces sliced fresh shiitake or button mushrooms (about 2¼ cups)
1 tablespoon grated fresh ginger
1 clove garlic, minced
1 tablespoon cooking oil
1 16-ounce package frozen sugar snap stir-fry vegetables
2 ounces dried udon noodles or spaghetti, broken
1 tablespoon snipped fresh cilantro

1 In a large saucepan bring the broth to boiling. Meanwhile, in a medium bowl gently stir together tofu cubes, soy sauce, and sesame oil; set aside.

2 In a medium saucepan cook the sliced mushrooms, ginger, and garlic in hot oil over medium-high heat for 4 minutes. Add to the hot broth.

3 Stir the frozen vegetables and udon noodles into the hot broth mixture. Bring to boiling; reduce heat. Simmer, covered, for 10 to 12 minutes or until vegetables and noodles are tender, stirring once or twice. Gently stir in the tofu mixture and the cilantro; heat through.

Nutrition Facts per serving: 175 cal., 9 g total fat (1 g sat. fat), 0 mg chol., 1,193 mg sodium, 17 g carbo., 2 g fiber, 10 g pro.
Daily Values: 33% vit. A, 21% vit. C, 5% calcium, 8% iron

tofu types

Tofu, sometimes called soybean curd or bean curd, is made by adding calcium to soy milk until it curdles. Much like cheese, the curds are then strained and pressed into cubes of varying firmness, depending on how much liquid is pressed out. When using tofu, match the firmness to the recipe. Soft or silken varieties blend into creamy consistencies for dips and sauces. Medium and firm tofu are best crumbled in soups as well as casseroles, salads, burgers, and stuffings. Use firm tofu for stir-frying and grilling.

Greek Minestrone ♥

Arborio rice is an Italian-grown grain that is shorter and plumper than other short-grain rice. Traditionally used to make creamy risotto, it adds a similar texture to this bean and vegetable soup.

Start to finish: 40 minutes **Makes:** 6 servings (about 10½ cups)

2 stalks celery, finely
   chopped
1 large onion, finely
   chopped (1 cup)
2 cloves garlic, minced
1 tablespoon olive oil
5 cups vegetable broth
1 cup water
½ cup uncooked arborio rice
6 cups torn spinach
1 15-ounce can Great
   Northern beans, rinsed
   and drained
3 medium tomatoes,
   chopped (about 2 cups)
1 medium zucchini, coarsely
   chopped (about
   1½ cups)
¼ cup snipped fresh thyme
¼ teaspoon cracked black
   pepper
½ cup crumbled feta cheese
   (2 ounces)

1 In a Dutch oven cook celery, onion, and garlic in hot oil over medium heat until tender. Add broth, water, and rice. Bring to boiling; reduce heat. Simmer, covered, for 15 minutes.

2 Add spinach, beans, tomatoes, zucchini, thyme, and pepper. Cook and stir until heated through. Ladle soup into bowls. Sprinkle each serving with cheese.

Nutrition Facts per serving: 252 cal., 6 g total fat (2 g sat. fat), 8 mg chol., 984 mg sodium, 39 g carbo., 8 g fiber, 13 g pro.
Daily Values: 44% vit. A, 58% vit. C, 15% calcium, 31% iron

Caramelized Onion Soup

Sweet onions and shallots are cooked to a luscious golden brown, intensifying their naturally tantalizing goodness.

Prep: 25 minutes **Cook:** 30 minutes **Makes:** 6 servings (about 7 cups)

3 pounds sweet onions, such as Vidalia, Walla Walla, or Maui
3 tablespoons olive oil or butter
12 medium shallots, halved (about 12 ounces)
4 cups vegetable broth
2 tablespoons dry white wine (optional)
6 ½-inch-thick slices sourdough or French bread (about 4 ounces)
6 ounces Gouda or Edam cheese, thinly sliced
Green onion tops (optional)

1 Cut about ½ inch off the tops of three of the whole onions. Peel off the papery outer leaves. Trim the root ends but leave them intact. Turn one of these onions so it rests on its top. Cut two thin (about ¼-inch) slices from the center of the onion, cutting down from the root end to the onion top. Be careful to keep these slices intact. Repeat with remaining 2 onions for a total of 6 thin, center-cut onion slices. Set remaining onions aside.

2 In a large skillet heat 1 tablespoon of the oil. Carefully add the 6 onion slices in a single layer. Cook, uncovered, over medium heat for 3 to 4 minutes or until golden brown. Turn carefully with a wide metal spatula. Cook about 3 minutes more or until golden brown on second side. Carefully remove from skillet and drain on paper towels.

3 Thinly slice remaining onion portions. Halve, peel, and cut remaining whole onions into thin slices. You should have 6 to 7 cups onion slices. In a 4- or 4½-quart Dutch oven heat the remaining 2 tablespoons oil over medium heat. Stir in the sliced onions and halved shallots. Cook, uncovered, over medium heat for 20 to 25 minutes or until onions are tender, stirring occasionally. Increase heat to medium-high and cook about 5 minutes or until onions are golden brown, stirring occasionally.

4 Stir broth and wine (if using) into onions in Dutch oven. Heat through. Season to taste with salt and black pepper.

5 Meanwhile, place bread slices on rack of broiler pan. Place under broiler, about 4 inches from the heat, about 1 minute or until lightly toasted. Turn bread over; top each piece with a slice of cheese. Broil for 1 to 2 minutes or just until cheese begins to melt.

6 To serve, ladle soup into bowls. Top each with a piece of cheese toast; add a caramelized onion slice and, if desired, a green onion top.

Nutrition Facts per serving: 333 cal., 13 g total fat (6 g sat. fat), 32 mg chol., 1,118 mg sodium, 41 g carbo., 4 g fiber, 14 g pro.
Daily Values: 17% vit. A, 28% vit. C, 26% calcium, 11% iron

Hot-and-Sour Tofu Soup ♥ FAST

The smooth-textured cubes of tofu contrast well with the crisp-tender vegetables and absorb the piquant flavors of rice vinegar, soy sauce, and fresh ginger.

Start to finish: 30 minutes **Makes:** 6 servings (about 8¼ cups)

- 3 14-ounce cans vegetable broth
- 3 tablespoons rice vinegar or white vinegar
- 2 tablespoons reduced-sodium soy sauce
- 2 teaspoons grated fresh ginger
- 1 teaspoon sugar
- ¼ to ½ teaspoon black pepper
- 2 cups thinly sliced fresh mushrooms
- 1 12- to 16-ounce package firm tofu (fresh bean curd), drained and cubed
- 1 8-ounce can sliced bamboo shoots, drained
- 1 8-ounce can sliced water chestnuts, drained
- 2 tablespoons cold water
- 2 tablespoons cornstarch
- 4 green onions, thinly sliced (½ cup)
- 2 eggs, beaten

1 In a 4-quart Dutch oven combine broth, vinegar, soy sauce, ginger, sugar, and pepper. Bring to boiling; reduce heat. Simmer, covered, for 2 minutes. Add mushrooms. Return to boiling; reduce heat. Simmer, covered, for 2 minutes more. Add tofu, bamboo shoots, and water chestnuts. Return to boiling.

2 Meanwhile, in a small bowl stir together the cold water and cornstarch. Stir cornstarch mixture into tofu mixture in Dutch oven. Cook and stir until slightly thickened and bubbly. Cook and stir for 2 minutes more. Stir in green onions. Pour the eggs into the soup in a steady stream while stirring 2 or 3 times to create shreds. Serve immediately.

Nutrition Facts per serving: 150 cal., 6 g total fat (1 g sat. fat), 71 mg chol., 1,074 mg sodium, 19 g carbo., 1 g fiber, 10 g pro.
Daily Values: 7% vit. A, 7% vit. C, 13% calcium, 8% iron

rice vinegar

Rice vinegar, made from rice wine or sake, has a subtle tang and a slightly sweet taste. Chinese rice vinegars are stronger than Japanese vinegars, although both are slightly milder than most vinegars. Chinese vinegars come in three types: white (clear or pale yellow), used mainly in hot-and-sour or sweet-and-sour dishes; red, a typical accompaniment for boiled or steamed shellfish; and black, used mainly as a condiment.

Winter Vegetable Soup ♥

Let these stick-to-the-ribs vegetables simmer all day long in your slow cooker. You'll welcome a steaming bowl of the chill-busting soup at the end of the day.

Prep: 30 minutes **Cook:** 10 hours **Makes:** 6 servings (about 8 cups)

2 medium parsnips, peeled, halved lengthwise, and cut into 1-inch pieces
1 large onion, chopped (1 cup)
1 medium turnip, peeled and cut into ¾-inch pieces
1 medium potato, cut into ¾-inch pieces
2 cups water
1 14½-ounce can diced tomatoes, undrained
¼ cup dry red wine or water
1 teaspoon salt
½ teaspoon dried thyme, crushed
¼ teaspoon dried sage, crushed
¼ teaspoon dried rosemary, crushed
4 cloves garlic, minced
2 15-ounce cans Great Northern or navy beans, rinsed and drained
¼ cup snipped fresh parsley

1 In a 3½- or 4-quart slow cooker place the parsnips, onion, turnip, and potato. Stir in water, undrained tomatoes, wine, salt, thyme, sage, rosemary, and garlic. Stir in beans.

2 Cover and cook on low-heat setting for 10 to 11 hours or on high-heat setting for 4½ to 5 hours. Stir in parsley just before serving.

Nutrition Facts per serving: 211 cal., 1 g total fat (0 g sat. fat), 0 mg chol., 853 mg sodium, 41 g carbo., 11 g fiber, 9 g pro.
Daily Values: 3% vit. A, 44% vit. C, 18% calcium, 18% iron

Tortellini and Vegetable Soup ♥

Cheese-stuffed tortellini, nutty wild rice, crisp-tender vegetables, and bits of robust dried tomato offer a variety of textures and flavors in each steaming bowl of this flavorful soup.

Prep: 20 minutes **Cook:** 45 minutes **Makes:** 4 servings (about 8 cups)

¼ cup wild rice
1 large onion, chopped (1 cup)
½ cup thinly sliced celery
3 cloves garlic, minced
1 tablespoon butter
4 14-ounce cans vegetable broth
1 teaspoon dried oregano, crushed
½ teaspoon dried marjoram, crushed
⅛ teaspoon black pepper
1 bay leaf
1 9-ounce package refrigerated cheese tortellini
2 cups chopped broccoli florets
¼ cup snipped dried tomatoes (not oil-packed)

1 Rinse wild rice in a strainer under cold running water about 1 minute. Drain; set aside.

2 In a 4-quart Dutch oven cook onion, celery, and garlic in hot butter over medium heat until vegetables are crisp-tender. Carefully stir in wild rice, broth, oregano, marjoram, pepper, and bay leaf. Bring to boiling; reduce heat. Simmer, covered, about 40 minutes or until rice is nearly tender. Discard bay leaf.

3 Add tortellini, broccoli, and dried tomatoes. Return to boiling; reduce heat. Cook, uncovered, for 5 to 6 minutes more or until tortellini and broccoli are just tender.

Nutrition Facts per serving: 336 cal., 10 g total fat (3 g sat. fat), 38 mg chol., 2,020 mg sodium, 51 g carbo., 4 g fiber, 17 g pro.
Daily Values: 24% vit. A, 78% vit. C, 17% calcium, 15% iron

Root Vegetable and Bean Soup ♥

Dig root vegetables? Then this bean soup is for you. The herb-seasoned broth is stocked with subterranean specialties—potatoes, parsnips, rutabaga, and carrots—made succulent via roasting.

Start to finish: 40 minutes **Makes:** 4 servings (about 8½ cups)

2 medium parsnips, peeled and cut into ½-inch pieces (1½ cups)

1 medium potato, cut into ½-inch pieces (1 cup)

1 small rutabaga, peeled and cut into ½-inch pieces (1 cup)

2 medium carrots, sliced ½ inch thick

1 medium onion, cut into 8 wedges

1 tablespoon olive oil

½ teaspoon sea salt or kosher salt

3 cups vegetable or chicken broth

1 15-ounce can small red beans, garbanzo beans (chickpeas), or Great Northern beans, rinsed and drained

2 teaspoons snipped fresh thyme

1 In a large roasting pan toss parsnips, potato, rutabaga, carrots, and onion with oil; sprinkle with salt. Spread the vegetables in a single layer in the roasting pan. Roast in a 450° oven for 15 to 20 minutes or until the vegetables start to brown.

2 Meanwhile, in a large saucepan bring broth and beans to boiling; add roasted vegetables. Return to boiling; reduce heat. Simmer, covered, about 5 minutes or until vegetables are tender. Stir in thyme. (For a thicker consistency, slightly mash vegetables and beans.)

Nutrition Facts per serving: 274 cal., 5 g total fat (1 g sat. fat), 0 mg chol., 1,338 mg sodium, 58 g carbo., 13 g fiber, 11 g pro.
Daily Values: 150% vit. A, 44% vit. C, 8% calcium, 22% iron

Potato-Curry Soup ♥

Curry powder and fresh ginger make this a tongue-tingling potato soup. Serve it with a cooling fruit salad for a meal with a pleasing contrast of taste, temperature, and texture.

Prep: 30 minutes **Cook:** 25 minutes **Makes:** 6 servings (about 9½ cups)

1 large onion, chopped (1 cup)
1 stalk celery, chopped
2 tablespoons bottled minced garlic
1 teaspoon grated fresh ginger
1 tablespoon butter
5 cups vegetable broth
4 medium potatoes, peeled and chopped (4 cups)
2 teaspoons curry powder
¼ teaspoon chili powder
1 12-ounce can (1½ cups) evaporated milk
¼ cup all-purpose flour
2 tablespoons snipped fresh parsley

1 In a large saucepan cook onion, celery, garlic, and ginger in hot butter over medium heat for 4 to 5 minutes. Carefully add broth, potatoes, curry powder, and chili powder. Bring to boiling; reduce heat. Simmer, covered, about 20 minutes or until potatoes are tender. Mash potatoes slightly.

2 Meanwhile, in screw-top jar combine ½ cup of the milk and the flour; cover and shake until smooth. Add flour mixture and remaining milk to soup in saucepan. Cook and stir until thickened and bubbly. Cook and stir for 1 minute more. Season to taste with salt and black pepper. Ladle soup into bowls. Sprinkle with parsley.

Nutrition Facts per serving: 236 cal., 8 g total fat (4 g sat. fat), 22 mg chol., 950 mg sodium, 30 g carbo., 3 g fiber, 12 g pro.
Daily Values: 7% vit. A, 32% vit. C, 18% calcium, 11% iron

Spring Vegetable Soup ♥ FAST

This is one super meal-in-a-bowl. Served in hollowed loaves of bread, this elegant potage scores high points for presentation—just the ticket for a casual get-together or family celebration.

Start to finish: 25 minutes **Makes:** 4 servings (about 6 cups)

2 14-ounce cans vegetable broth (3½ cups)
1 8-ounce can water chestnuts, drained and coarsely chopped
2 ounces dried angel hair pasta, broken (about 1 cup)
½ teaspoon snipped fresh savory or thyme
2 tablespoons cornstarch
8 ounces asparagus spears, cut into 1-inch pieces
½ cup frozen peas
2 tablespoons snipped fresh mint
4 5-inch bread bowls* or sliced French bread

1 In a medium saucepan combine 3 cups of the broth, the water chestnuts, pasta, and savory. Bring to boiling; reduce heat. Simmer, covered, for 5 minutes.

2 In a small bowl stir together the remaining ½ cup broth and the cornstarch; add to saucepan. Stir in asparagus and peas. Cook and stir until thickened and bubbly. Cook and stir for 2 minutes more or until vegetables are tender and pasta is tender but firm. Stir in the mint.

3 To serve, ladle soup into bread bowls or serve in soup bowls with French bread.

Nutrition Facts per serving: 268 cal., 3 g total fat (0 g sat. fat), 0 mg chol., 1,203 mg sodium, 56 g carbo., 2 g fiber, 9 g pro.
Daily Values: 6% vit. A, 23% vit. C, 5% calcium, 23% iron

*Note: To make bread bowls, hollow out small round loaves, leaving ½-inch-thick shells. If desired, brush the insides with 2 tablespoons melted butter. Bake in a 350° oven for 10 minutes or until lightly toasted.

slow cooker conversions

With a little tweaking, you can cook many of your favorite soups and stews in your slow cooker. Here are a few hints for adjusting recipes.

Choosing a recipe Use recipes that call for less-tender cuts of meat, such as beef chuck roast, beef brisket, pork shoulder, and stew meat. Find a recipe in this book that is similar to yours. Use this sample recipe as a guide to estimate ingredient quantities and timings.

Quantities The slow cooker must be at least half full and no more than two-thirds full. If necessary, add an extra potato, carrot, or onion to fill the cooker to the halfway point.

Vegetables Cut potatoes, carrots, parsnips, and other dense vegetables into bite-size pieces; place them in the bottom of the cooker. Add tender vegetables such as fresh or frozen broccoli, green beans, or peas near the end of the cooking time and cook on the high-heat setting 30 minutes or until tender.

Meat Trim any fat from the meat and cut in half roasts larger than 2½ pounds. If desired, brown the meat. Place the meat on top of the vegetables.

Poultry Remove skin from poultry pieces before cooking.

Ground meats, poultry, and sausage Brown all ground meats, poultry, and sausage in a skillet over medium heat. These products must be completely cooked before you place them in the slow cooker.

Liquids Reduce by about half the total amount of the liquid in your recipe.

Thickening Use quick-cooking tapioca for thickening stews and sauces, or thicken the juices with cornstarch and flour in a saucepan at the end of cooking. For each cup of liquid, use 1 tablespoon cornstarch or 2 tablespoons all-purpose flour.

Dairy products Milk, cream, and natural cheeses break down when cooked for long periods of time. Canned condensed cream soups and packaged white sauce mixes can be used to add creaminess. Evaporated milk also can be used, if you add it during the last 30 to 60 minutes of cooking time. Stir cheese into the finished dish just before serving.

Dry beans Rinse beans and place in a saucepan. Add enough water to cover beans by 2 inches. Bring to boiling; reduce heat. Simmer, uncovered, for 10 minutes. Remove from heat. Cover and let stand about 1 hour. Drain and rinse beans before adding them to the slow cooker.

Emerald Soup

The glorious green shade of this soup comes from spinach and watercress. A hint of lemon provides a fresh taste, while ground red pepper adds a gentle kick.

Start to finish: 40 minutes **Makes:** 6 to 8 servings (about 6 cups)

5 green onions, chopped (⅔ cup)
4 large cloves garlic, minced
2 tablespoons butter
2 tablespoons all-purpose flour
3 cups vegetable broth
3½ cups half-and-half or light cream
1 teaspoon finely shredded lemon peel
¼ teaspoon ground white pepper
¼ teaspoon ground nutmeg
⅛ teaspoon ground red pepper
6 cups fresh spinach leaves, chopped
1 cup watercress, chopped

1 In a large saucepan cook green onions and garlic in hot butter over medium heat for 3 to 5 minutes or until onions are tender. Stir in flour and cook for 2 minutes. Carefully stir or whisk in broth. Cook and stir or whisk about 5 minutes or until thoroughly combined and slightly thickened.

2 Add half-and-half, lemon peel, white pepper, nutmeg, red pepper, spinach, and watercress. Bring to a gentle boil; reduce heat. Simmer, covered, about 10 minutes or until spinach and watercress are tender.

3 Place half of the spinach mixture in a blender container or food processor bowl. Cover and blend or process until smooth. Repeat with remaining mixture. Return all of the mixture to the saucepan; heat through.

Nutrition Facts per serving: 263 cal., 21 g total fat (13 g sat. fat), 63 mg chol., 643 mg sodium, 11 g carbo., 2 g fiber, 9 g pro.
Daily Values: 64% vit. A, 37% vit. C, 18% calcium, 14% iron

Potato-Beet Soup ♥

This playful, colorful soup will surely brighten a winter evening. The ruby red beets and cream-colored potatoes blend to a lovely shade of rose.

Prep: 15 minutes. **Cook:** 30 minutes. **Makes:** 4 servings (about 5 cups)

2 medium potatoes, peeled
    and cubed (12 ounces)
2 leeks, coarsely chopped
    (⅔ cup)
1 tablespoon olive oil
4 teaspoons all-purpose
    flour
2½ cups vegetable broth
½ teaspoon dried basil,
    crushed
½ teaspoon dried savory,
    crushed
½ teaspoon dried tarragon,
    crushed
½ of a 16-ounce jar Harvard
    beets and their liquid
    (about ¾ cup)
½ cup half-and-half, light
    cream, or whipping
    cream
    Fried potato strips
    (optional)

1 In a medium saucepan cook potatoes and leeks in hot oil over medium heat for 3 minutes. Stir in flour. Carefully add broth, basil, savory, and tarragon. Bring to boiling, stirring occasionally; reduce heat. Simmer, covered, about 20 minutes or until potatoes are very tender. Stir in beets. Cool slightly.

2 Place half of the potato mixture in a blender container or food processor bowl. Cover and blend or process until smooth. Repeat with remaining potato mixture. Return all of the potato mixture to the saucepan. Stir in half-and-half; heat through. If desired, top with fried potato strips.

Nutrition Facts per serving: 229 cal., 8 g total fat (3 g sat. fat), 12 mg chol., 722 mg sodium, 34 g carbo., 3 g fiber, 7 g pro.
Daily Values: 4% vit. A, 17% vit. C, 6% calcium, 11% iron

Lentil-Spinach Soup ♥

Lentils have a mild nutty taste, a beanlike texture, and plenty of protein. And unlike beans, lentils don't need soaking—an added benefit for time-pressed cooks.

Prep: 25 minutes **Cook:** 50 minutes **Makes:** 4 servings (about 8 cups)

1 medium onion, chopped (½ cup)
4 cloves garlic, minced
2 tablespoons cooking oil
3 14-ounce cans (5¼ cups) vegetable broth
1 14½-ounce can diced tomatoes, undrained
1 cup dry lentils, rinsed and drained
2 teaspoons ground cumin
1½ teaspoons ground coriander
1 teaspoon paprika
¼ teaspoon black pepper
1 10-ounce package frozen chopped spinach, thawed and drained
1 tablespoon lemon juice

1 In a large saucepan cook onion and garlic in hot oil over medium heat until tender. Stir in broth, undrained tomatoes, lentils, cumin, coriander, paprika, and pepper. Bring to boiling; reduce heat. Simmer, covered, for 45 minutes.

2 Stir in spinach and lemon juice. Cook, uncovered, for 5 minutes more.

Nutrition Facts per serving: 307 cal., 8 g total fat (1 g sat. fat), 0 mg chol., 1,366 mg sodium, 40 g carbo., 18 g fiber, 20 g pro.
Daily Values: 212% vit. A, 40% vit. C, 14% calcium, 26% iron

Veggie Soup with Curry Croutons ♥

Pureeing a combination of root vegetables—fennel, turnip, potato, and carrot—provides a flavorful base for this bean soup. For a golden crowning touch, sprinkle with the optional croutons.

Prep: 25 minutes   **Bake:** 15 minutes   **Cook:** 25 minutes   **Makes:** 4 servings (about 5 cups)

1 medium fennel bulb
   (4 to 5 ounces)
¼ cup chopped onion
1 clove garlic, minced
2 teaspoons cooking oil
3 cups vegetable broth
1 medium turnip, peeled
   and cubed (about
   ¾ cup)
1 medium potato, peeled
   and cubed (about
   ⅔ cup)
1 medium carrot, sliced
   (½ cup)
¼ teaspoon ground white
   or black pepper
1 15- or 19-ounce can white
   kidney (cannellini)
   beans, rinsed and
   drained
¼ cup half-and-half or light
   cream
1 recipe Curry Croutons
   (optional)

1 Cut off and discard upper stalks of fennel, snipping and reserving feathery leaves for garnish. Remove any wilted outer layers of fennel and discard; remove core. Finely chop remaining fennel; set aside.

2 In a large saucepan cook onion and garlic in hot oil over medium heat about 5 minutes or until onion is tender. Carefully add chopped fennel, broth, turnip, potato, carrot, and pepper. Bring to boiling; reduce heat. Simmer, covered, for 25 to 30 minutes or until vegetables are very tender. Cool slightly.

3 Place one-third of the vegetable mixture in a blender container or food processor bowl. Cover and blend or process until smooth. Repeat twice with remaining mixture. Return all of the mixture to saucepan. Stir in beans and half-and-half. Heat through; do not boil. Season to taste with salt.

4 To serve, ladle soup into bowls. If desired, float a few Curry Croutons on each serving. Garnish with snipped fennel leaves.

Nutrition Facts per serving: 282 cal., 10 g total fat (2 g sat. fat), 6 mg chol., 1,103 mg sodium, 42 g carbo., 16 g fiber, 14 g pro.
Daily Values: 42% vit. A, 20% vit. C, 8% calcium, 17% iron

Curry Croutons: In a medium bowl combine 1 tablespoon olive oil and ½ teaspoon curry powder. Tear three ¾-inch slices Italian bread into bite-size pieces. Add the torn bread pieces to the oil mixture; toss until coated. Spread bread pieces in a single layer in a 15×10×1-inch baking pan. Bake in a 350° oven for 15 to 20 minutes or until croutons begin to brown, stirring once.

Split Pea Soup with Spiced Yogurt

This vivid split pea soup gets an exotic East Indian flair from yogurt spiced with turmeric, cumin, and ground red pepper.

Prep: 15 minutes **Cook:** 1¼ hours **Makes:** 4 servings (about 6 cups)

1 cup dry split peas
4 cups vegetable broth
¼ teaspoon dried rosemary, crushed
1 bay leaf
1 medium onion, chopped (½ cup)
2 stalks celery, sliced (1 cup)
2 medium carrots, chopped (1 cup)
2 cloves garlic, minced
2 tablespoons dry sherry
½ cup plain low-fat yogurt
¼ teaspoon ground turmeric
¼ teaspoon paprika
¼ teaspoon ground cumin
⅛ teaspoon ground red pepper

1 Rinse split peas. In a large saucepan combine peas, broth, rosemary, and bay leaf. Bring to boiling; reduce heat. Simmer, covered, for 1 hour, stirring occasionally.

2 Stir in onion, celery, carrots, and garlic. Return to boiling; reduce heat. Simmer, covered, for 15 to 20 minutes more or until vegetables are crisp-tender. Discard bay leaf. Stir in sherry.

3 Meanwhile, in a small bowl stir together yogurt, turmeric, paprika, cumin, and red pepper.

4 To serve, ladle soup into bowls. Top each serving with some of the yogurt mixture.

Nutrition Facts per serving: 266 cal., 3 g total fat (1 g sat. fat), 2 mg chol., 852 mg sodium, 40 g carbo., 2 g fiber, 20 g pro.
Daily Values: 99% vit. A, 15% vit. C, 15% calcium, 22% iron

Cheesy Cauliflower Chowder FAST

The rye bread is a snappy complement to the rich, nutty, buttery flavor of the Jarlsberg cheese. Toss mixed greens and sliced pears with a citrus vinaigrette for a salad to serve on the side.

Prep: 20 minutes **Cook:** 10 minutes **Makes:** 6 servings (about 8 cups)

1 large onion, chopped (1 cup)
2 tablespoons butter
4 cups vegetable broth
2 cups diced, peeled Yukon gold or white potatoes
2½ cups cauliflower florets
1 cup half-and-half, light cream, or milk
2 tablespoons all-purpose flour
2½ cups shredded Jarlsberg cheese (10 ounces)
3 slices dark rye or pumpernickel bread, halved crosswise (optional)
½ cup shredded Jarlsberg cheese (2 ounces) (optional)
2 tablespoons snipped fresh Italian flat-leaf parsley (optional)

1 In a large saucepan cook onion in hot butter over medium heat until tender. Carefully add broth and potatoes. Bring to boiling; reduce heat. Simmer, covered, for 6 minutes. Add cauliflower. Return to boiling; reduce heat. Simmer, covered, for 4 to 6 minutes more or until vegetables are tender.

2 In a bowl whisk half-and-half into flour until smooth; add to the soup mixture. Cook and stir until mixture is thickened and bubbly. Reduce heat to low. Stir in the 2½ cups cheese until melted. Do not allow the mixture to boil. Season to taste with salt and black pepper.

3 If using bread, trim crusts from bread. Place the halved bread slices on a baking sheet. Bake in a 350° oven about 3 minutes or until crisp on top. Turn slices over. If desired, sprinkle with the ½ cup cheese and the parsley. Bake about 5 minutes more or until cheese melts.

4 Ladle soup into bowls. If desired, float one piece of cheese-topped bread in each bowl of soup.

Nutrition Facts per serving: 267 cal., 17 g total fat (12 g sat. fat), 58 mg chol., 682 mg sodium, 14 g carbo., 2 g fiber, 15 g pro.
Daily Values: 15% vit. A, 31% vit. C, 39% calcium, 5% iron

Corn and Cheese Chowder FAST

Keep a handful of foods stocked in your pantry and refrigerator so you can whip up this family-pleasing soup in minutes.

Start to finish: 10 minutes **Makes:** 4 servings (about 6 cups)

1   14-ounce can vegetable broth
1   10-ounce package frozen whole kernel corn
1   4½-ounce can diced green chile peppers, drained
½   teaspoon chili powder
2   cups milk
3   tablespoons all-purpose flour
1   cup shredded American cheese (4 ounces)

1 In a large saucepan combine broth, corn, chile peppers, and chili powder. Bring to boiling; reduce heat. Simmer, covered, for 5 minutes.

2 In a screw-top jar combine ½ cup of the milk and the flour; cover and shake until smooth. Stir flour mixture and remaining milk into hot mixture in the saucepan. Cook and stir over medium heat until mixture is slightly thickened and bubbly. Cook and stir for 1 minute more. Stir in cheese until melted.

Nutrition Facts per serving: 273 cal., 13 g total fat (1 g sat. fat), 36 mg chol., 976 mg sodium, 27 g carbo., 0 g fiber, 16 g pro.
Daily Values: 20% vit. A, 22% vit. C, 30% calcium, 8% iron

Vegetable Chili with Cheese

A cheddar-and-chive cream cheese topping adds a soothing counterpoint to this spunky chili. Use it to cool the fire in other chilies too.

Prep: 20 minutes **Cook:** 45 minutes **Makes:** 5 servings (about 7 cups)

Nonstick cooking spray
1¼ cups finely chopped zucchini
¾ cup finely chopped carrot
2 tablespoons sliced green onion
2 cloves garlic, minced
2 15-ounce cans hot-style chili beans in chili sauce, undrained
2 14½-ounce cans diced tomatoes, undrained
1 tablespoon unsweetened cocoa powder
1 teaspoon chili powder
1 teaspoon ground cumin
1 teaspoon bottled hot pepper sauce (optional)
¼ teaspoon dried oregano, crushed
½ of an 8-ounce tub cream cheese with chive and onion (½ cup)
2 tablespoons milk
½ cup shredded cheddar cheese (2 ounces)
Green onion strips (optional)

1 Lightly coat a large saucepan with cooking spray. Add zucchini, carrot, sliced green onion, and garlic to saucepan. Cook over medium heat for 2 minutes. Add undrained chili beans, undrained tomatoes, cocoa powder, chili powder, cumin, hot pepper sauce (if desired), and oregano. Bring to boiling; reduce heat. Simmer, uncovered, over low heat about 40 minutes or until desired consistency, stirring occasionally.

2 Meanwhile, for cheese topping, in a small bowl stir together cream cheese and milk until smooth. Stir in cheddar cheese. Ladle chili into bowls. Spoon a little cheese topping onto each serving of chili. If desired, garnish with green onion.

Nutrition Facts per serving: 328 cal., 13 g total fat (7 g sat. fat), 32 mg chol., 1,132 mg sodium, 41 g carbo., 11 g fiber, 14 g pro.
Daily Values: 105% vit. A, 44% vit. C, 26% calcium, 21% iron

Two-Bean Chili ♥

Calling all hearty appetites! This satisfying blend of black beans, white kidney beans, jicama, and chile peppers boasts a pronounced south-of-the-border flavor.

Start to finish: 35 minutes **Makes:** 4 servings (about 5 cups)

1 medium onion, chopped
 (½ cup)
1 clove garlic, minced
1 tablespoon cooking oil
1 15-ounce can white kidney
 (cannellini) beans,
 rinsed and drained
1 15-ounce can black beans,
 rinsed and drained
1 14-ounce can vegetable
 broth
1 cup chopped peeled
 jicama or potato
1 4-ounce can diced green
 chile peppers,
 undrained
1 teaspoon ground cumin
2 tablespoons snipped fresh
 cilantro
1 tablespoon lime juice
¼ cup crumbled queso
 fresco or feta cheese
 (1 ounce)

1 In a large saucepan cook onion and garlic in hot oil over medium heat until tender. Stir in white kidney beans, black beans, broth, jicama or potato, undrained chile peppers, and cumin. Bring to boiling; reduce heat. Simmer, covered, about 10 minutes or until jicama is crisp-tender or potato is tender.

2 Stir cilantro and lime juice into bean mixture; heat through. Ladle chili into bowls. Top with cheese.

Nutrition Facts per serving: 254 cal., 9 g total fat (3 g sat. fat), 15 mg chol., 1,110 mg sodium, 37 g carbo., 10 g fiber, 19 g pro.
Daily Values: 2% vit. A, 32% vit. C, 16% calcium, 24% iron

White Bean and Cumin Chili

Toasting the cumin seeds brings out the deep, nutty flavor. You'll know the cumin is ready when your kitchen fills with a fragrant aroma.

Prep: 30 minutes **Cook:** 1 hour **Makes:** 4 servings (about 8 cups)

1 large onion, chopped
    (1 cup)
3 cloves garlic, minced
2 tablespoons cooking oil
2 14½-ounce cans diced
    tomatoes, undrained
1 12-ounce can beer or
    nonalcoholic beer
1 chipotle chile pepper in
    adobo sauce, chopped
1 tablespoon cumin seeds,
    toasted and ground*
1 teaspoon sugar
½ teaspoon salt
2 19-ounce cans baby or
    regular cannellini or
    white navy beans, rinsed
    and drained
1½ cups coarsely chopped,
    seeded, and peeled
    golden nugget,
    butternut, and/or acorn
    squash (about
    12 ounces)
½ cup dairy sour cream
2 tablespoons lime juice
1 tablespoon snipped fresh
    chives
   Whole fresh chives
    (optional)
   Small lime wedges
    (optional)

1 In a 4-quart Dutch oven cook onion and garlic in hot oil over medium heat until onion is tender. Stir in the undrained tomatoes, beer, chipotle pepper, cumin seeds, sugar, and salt. Stir in beans. Bring to boiling; reduce heat. Stir in squash. Simmer, covered, for 1 hour.

2 Meanwhile, combine sour cream, lime juice, and snipped chives. To serve, ladle chili into bowls. Top with the sour cream mixture. If desired, garnish with fresh chives and small lime wedges.

Nutrition Facts per serving: 365 cal., 15 g total fat (5 g. sat. fat), 13 mg chol., 995 mg sodium, 52 g carbo., 13 g fiber, 17 g pro.
Daily Values: 26% vit. A, 67% vit. C, 15% calcium, 33% iron

*Note: To toast cumin seeds, place seeds in a dry skillet over low heat. Cook, stirring often, about 8 minutes or until seeds become fragrant. (Avoid overcooking, which can make the seeds bitter.) Remove from heat; allow to cool before grinding with a food mill or a mortar and pestle.

Garbanzo Bean Stew FAST

No need to wait for cool weather to serve this colorful stew. It's a satisfying meal any time of the year. The feta cheese—an optional addition—lends a tangy, fresh flavor.

Start to finish: 20 minutes **Makes:** 4 servings (about 6½ cups)

 1 large onion, chopped
      (1 cup)
 1 medium green sweet
      pepper, chopped
 3 cloves garlic, minced
 1 tablespoon cooking oil
1½ teaspoons ground cumin
 ½ teaspoon paprika
 ⅛ to ¼ teaspoon ground red
      pepper
 2 14-ounce cans vegetable
      broth
 1 10-ounce package
      (2 cups) frozen whole
      kernel corn
 1 15-ounce can garbanzo
      beans (chickpeas),
      rinsed and drained
 1 medium tomato, chopped
 2 tablespoons snipped fresh
      oregano
 2 tablespoons lemon juice
 2 tablespoons thinly sliced
      green onion
 ¼ cup crumbled feta cheese
      (optional)

1 In a covered large saucepan cook onion, sweet pepper, and garlic in hot oil over medium heat until onion is tender, stirring occasionally. Stir in cumin, paprika, and ground red pepper; cook for 1 minute.

2 Carefully add broth and frozen corn. Bring to boiling; reduce heat. Simmer, covered, for 5 to 10 minutes or until corn is tender. Stir in beans, tomato, oregano, and lemon juice. Heat through. Ladle into bowls. Sprinkle with green onion and, if desired, cheese.

Nutrition Facts per serving: 246 cal., 7 g total fat (1 g sat. fat), 0 mg chol., 1,169 mg sodium, 42 g carbo., 8 g fiber, 10 g pro.
Daily Values: 12% vit. A, 65% vit. C, 7% calcium, 9% iron

Herb and Pepper Lentil Stew ♥

Look for pappadams, which are wafer-thin East Indian breads made with lentil flour, in Indian specialty markets or large supermarkets.

Prep: 10 minutes **Cook:** 30 minutes **Makes:** 4 servings (about 6 cups)

1	tablespoon cooking oil
2	medium onions, quartered
1	medium green sweet pepper, cut into ½-inch rings
1	tablespoon snipped fresh thyme or 1 teaspoon dried thyme, crushed
¼	teaspoon crushed red pepper
5	cups water
1¼	cups dried red (Egyptian) lentils*, rinsed and drained
1½	teaspoons salt
4	sprigs fresh thyme (optional)
	Pappadams, toasted (optional)

1 In a Dutch oven heat oil over medium-high heat for 30 seconds. Add onion quarters. Cook about 8 minutes or until brown, stirring occasionally.

2 Add sweet pepper, snipped thyme, and crushed red pepper. Cook and stir for 2 minutes. Remove from heat. Add water, 1 cup of lentils, and salt. Return to heat. Bring to boiling; reduce heat. Simmer, uncovered, for 15 minutes.

3 Add remaining lentils. Cook, uncovered, for 3 to 5 minutes more or until lentils are tender.

4 To serve, ladle stew into bowls. If desired, top with fresh thyme sprigs and serve with pappadams.

Nutrition Facts per serving: 246 cal., 4 g total fat (1 g sat. fat), 0 mg chol., 902 mg sodium, 39 g carbo., 10 g fiber, 15 g pro.
Daily Values: 3% vit. A, 41% vit. C, 6% calcium, 18% iron

***Note:** Brown or green lentils may be substituted for the red lentils. Prepare recipe as directed, except add all the lentils with water and salt. Bring to boiling; reduce heat. Simmer, covered, for 25 minutes. Uncover. Simmer for 5 minutes more.

Bean and Brussels Sprouts Stew ♥

This extraordinary vegetable stew begs for crusty bread to mop up any juices remaining at the bottom of the bowl.

Prep: 35 minutes **Cook:** 16 minutes **Makes:** 4 to 6 servings (about 6 cups)

Nonstick cooking spray

1 small onion, chopped (⅓ cup)

6 cloves garlic, minced

1 small fennel bulb, trimmed, cored, and thinly sliced (about 2 cups)

12 ounces acorn, butternut, or turban winter squash, seeded, peeled, and cut into ¾-inch pieces (about 2 cups)

8 ounces fresh Brussels sprouts, trimmed and halved (2 cups)

1 14-ounce can vegetable broth

⅓ cup dry white wine or apple juice

2 tablespoons snipped fresh sage, crushed

1 tablespoon snipped fresh rosemary or 1 teaspoon dried rosemary, crushed

1 tart cooking apple, cored and coarsely chopped (about 1 cup), or 6 dried apricots, quartered (about ¼ cup)

1 15-ounce can red kidney beans, rinsed and drained

1 tablespoon sherry vinegar or balsamic vinegar

1 tablespoon honey

1 Lightly coat a 4-quart Dutch oven with cooking spray. Add onion and garlic; cook and stir over medium heat for 5 minutes. Add fennel, squash, Brussels sprouts, broth, wine, sage, and rosemary. Bring to boiling; reduce heat. Simmer, covered, about 8 minutes or until vegetables are nearly tender.

2 Add apple. Cook, covered, about 3 minutes more or just until Brussels sprouts are tender. Add beans, vinegar, and honey; heat through. Season to taste with salt and fresh ground black pepper.

Nutrition Facts per serving: 213 cal., 2 g total fat (0 g sat. fat), 0 mg chol., 634 mg sodium, 45 g carbo., 22 g fiber, 11 g pro.
Daily Values: 50% vit. A, 90% vit. C, 18% iron

Chunky Ratatouille Stew ♥

Simmer the bounty of a summer garden into this stew. Like typical ratatouille, it combines eggplant, onion, sweet pepper, and your choice of green beans or zucchini.

Start to finish: 35 minutes **Makes:** 4 servings (about 6 cups)

1 large onion, chopped
  (1 cup)
1 cup chopped green sweet
  pepper
1 tablespoon olive oil
2 cups small whole fresh
  mushrooms (about
  6 ounces), stems
  removed
2 cups peeled and chopped
  eggplant (about
  6 ounces)
4 ounces green beans, cut
  into 1-inch pieces, or
  1 small zucchini, thinly
  sliced (about 1 cup)
2 cups vegetable broth
2 tablespoons dry red wine
1 14½-ounce can diced
  tomatoes with roasted
  garlic and red pepper,
  undrained
1 tablespoon snipped fresh
  basil
½ cup shredded provolone
  cheese (2 ounces)

1 In a Dutch oven cook the onion and sweet pepper in hot oil over medium heat until tender. Stir in the mushrooms, eggplant, and green beans. Add broth and wine. Bring to boiling; reduce heat. Simmer, covered, for 8 to 10 minutes or until vegetables are tender.

2 Stir in undrained tomatoes and basil; heat through. Ladle into bowls. Sprinkle with provolone cheese.

Nutrition Facts per serving: 163 cal., 8 g total fat (3 g sat. fat), 10 mg chol., 1,135 mg sodium, 16 g carbo., 3 g fiber, 8 g pro.
Daily Values: 13% vit. A, 65% vit. C, 14% calcium, 10% iron

Sides

Farmer's Vegetable Broth

In This Chapter:

Alpine Cheese Soup 176

Baby Vegetable Minestrone 181

Baked Potato Soup 168

Beet Borscht 162

Carrot and Chile
   Pepper Soup 180

Chilled Carrot Bisque 169

Chilled Peach-Yogurt Soup 184

Cream of Roasted
   Fennel Soup 160

Cumin Butternut
   Squash Soup 177

Easy Squash Soup 159

Farmer's Market
   Melon Soup 186

Farmer's Vegetable Broth 173

Fresh Mushroom Soup 175

Fresh Pea Soup 179

Gazpacho To Go 178

German Potato Soup 182

Gingered Pumpkin-
   Pear Soup 164

Iced Yellow Tomato Soup 172

Leek-Gruyère
   Cream Soup 171

Minestrone 161

Oysters Rockefeller Soup 166

Red Pepper Soup 165

Squash-Potato Chowder 167

Strawberry-Melon Soup 183

Sweet Potato and
   Pear Vichyssoise 170

Tutti-Frutti Spiced
   Fruit Soup 185

Two-Tomato Soup 158

Two-Tomato Soup

For the fullest flavor, choose the ripest fresh tomatoes you can find. If homegrown or farm-fresh tomatoes are available, they'll make the best soup.

Prep: 45 minutes **Cook:** 65 minutes **Makes:** 8 servings (about 8 cups)

1 3-ounce package dried tomatoes (not oil-packed)
1 tablespoon olive oil or cooking oil
1 medium onion, chopped (½ cup)
¼ teaspoon coarsely ground black pepper
8 medium fresh tomatoes, chopped (about 2½ pounds)
4 cups water
1 teaspoon salt
1 cup whipping cream
   Olive oil (optional)
8 yellow teardrop or dried yellow tomato halves (optional)

1 Place the dried tomatoes in a small bowl. Add enough boiling water to cover. Let stand for 30 minutes. Drain and rinse. Coarsely chop rehydrated tomatoes.

2 In a Dutch oven heat the 1 tablespoon oil. Cook and stir onion, rehydrated tomatoes, and pepper in hot oil over medium heat about 5 minutes or until onion is tender.

3 Measure ¾ cup of the chopped fresh tomatoes; set aside. Add remaining fresh tomatoes to rehydrated tomato mixture. Cook, covered, over low heat about 20 minutes or until tomatoes are soft. Add water and salt. Cook, uncovered, over low heat for 40 minutes more, stirring often.

4 Place one-fourth of the mixture in a blender container or food processor bowl. Cover and blend or process until smooth. Repeat 3 times with remaining mixture. Return all of the mixture to Dutch oven. Heat to simmering. Stir in cream. Return just to simmering. Remove from heat.

5 To serve, ladle soup into bowls. Spoon some of the reserved fresh chopped tomatoes into each bowl. If desired, drizzle each serving with some olive oil and top with a yellow teardrop or dried yellow tomato half.

Nutrition Facts per serving: 176 cal., 14 g total fat (7 g sat. fat), 41 mg chol., 540 mg sodium, 13 g carbo., 3 g fiber, 3 g pro.
Daily Values: 21% vit. A, 47% vit. C, 4% calcium, 9% iron

To Make Ahead: Prepare soup as directed up to adding the whipping cream. Cool soup. Transfer to an airtight container. Seal, label, and freeze up to 3 months. To reheat, transfer frozen soup to a saucepan. Cook, covered, over medium heat for 15 to 20 minutes, stirring occasionally. Stir in whipping cream. Cook and stir for 5 to 10 minutes more or until heated through.

Easy Squash Soup   FAST

Winter squash—blessed with a velvety texture, a buttery taste, plus a good amount of dietary fiber—makes a nutrient-packed soup base. Frozen squash makes this soup extra easy.

Prep: 5 minutes **Cook:** 10 minutes **Makes:** 4 servings (about 4 cups)

1½ teaspoons cooking oil
¼ cup finely chopped onion
1 to 2 teaspoons curry powder
½ teaspoon ground ginger
2 12-ounce packages frozen cooked winter squash, thawed
1 cup reduced-sodium chicken broth
1 cup apple juice or apple cider
¼ teaspoon salt
½ cup plain nonfat yogurt or nonfat dairy sour cream
   Finely chopped pistachio nuts (optional)

1 In a medium saucepan heat oil over medium heat. Add onion, curry powder, and ground ginger. Cook and stir for 2 minutes. Add the squash, broth, apple juice, and salt. Heat through.

2 To serve, ladle into bowls. Top each serving with a swirl of yogurt. If desired, sprinkle with nuts.

Nutrition Facts per serving: 142 cal., 3 g total fat (1 g sat. fat), 1 mg chol., 353 mg sodium, 26 g carbo., 5 g fiber, 5 g pro.
Daily Values: 60% vit. A, 29% vit. C, 7% calcium, 7% iron

Cream of Roasted Fennel Soup

This creamy, rich-tasting soup is surprisingly low in fat and calories. Make it ahead of time so you merely need to reheat and garnish it as everyone sits down to eat.

Prep: 20 minutes **Cook:** 25 minutes **Roast:** 25 minutes **Makes:** 8 servings (about 8 cups)

1 large fennel bulb (1½ to 2 pounds)
1 large white onion, coarsely chopped (1 cup)
2 teaspoons olive oil
½ teaspoon coarse salt
4 cups chicken or vegetable stock or broth
1 large russet potato, peeled and cut into ½-inch cubes
1 cup fat-free half-and-half or fat-free evaporated milk
2 tablespoons grapefruit juice
¾ teaspoon ground cumin
Ground white pepper
1 tablespoon fennel seeds
Edible flowers (optional)

1 Trim tough stalks and bottom stem from fennel bulb; reserve leafy tops. Cut the bulb and tender stalks into ½-inch slices.

2 Arrange fennel and onion in a 13×9×2-inch baking pan. Drizzle with olive oil and sprinkle with salt. Roast in a 375° oven for 25 minutes or just until the vegetables are tender but not brown.

3 Transfer roasted fennel and onion to a large saucepan. Add stock and potato. Bring to boiling; reduce heat. Simmer, covered, about 10 minutes or until vegetables are tender. Cool slightly.

4 Place one-third of the fennel mixture in a blender container or food processor bowl. Blend or process until smooth. Repeat twice with remaining fennel mixture. Return all of the mixture to saucepan. Stir in half-and-half, grapefruit juice, and cumin. Heat through. Season to taste with white pepper.

5 Meanwhile, place the fennel seeds in a small skillet over medium-high heat and toast about 3 minutes or until light brown and fragrant, stirring frequently.

6 To serve, ladle soup into bowls. Top each serving with a piece of fennel top and sprinkle with toasted fennel seeds. If desired, garnish with edible flowers.

Nutrition Facts per serving: 84 cal., 2 g total fat (0 g sat. fat), 44 mg chol., 534 mg sodium, 13 g carbo., 5 g fiber, 3 g pro.
Daily Values: 1% vit. A, 16% vit. C, 5% calcium, 3% iron

To Make Ahead: Prepare soup as directed; cool. Transfer to an airtight container. Refrigerate up to 2 days. Reheat gently in a covered saucepan before serving.

Minestrone

Minestrone takes many forms in Italy as well as stateside, but most versions feature white beans, pasta, and an assortment of seasonal vegetables. This one includes those ingredients, plus bacon.

Prep: 20 minutes **Cook:** 30 minutes **Makes:** 6 servings (about 12 cups)

10 cups water
1 15-ounce can white kidney (cannellini) beans or garbanzo beans (chickpeas), rinsed and drained
1 cup chopped carrots
1 cup chopped turnip
1 cup fresh green beans cut into 1-inch pieces
1 teaspoon salt
½ teaspoon black pepper
¼ teaspoon dried oregano, crushed
4 ounces dried spaghetti, broken into small pieces
3 slices bacon
1 large onion, chopped (1 cup)
1 cup chopped celery
2 cloves garlic, minced
1 14½-ounce can tomatoes, cut up and undrained
½ cup snipped fresh parsley (optional)

1 In a 4-quart Dutch oven or saucepan combine water, white kidney beans, carrots, turnip, green beans, salt, pepper, and oregano. Bring to boiling; reduce heat. Simmer, uncovered, for 30 minutes, adding spaghetti for the last 10 minutes of cooking.

2 Meanwhile, in a large skillet cook bacon until crisp and brown; remove from skillet, reserving drippings. Drain bacon on paper towels; cool.

3 Add onion, celery, and garlic to drippings in skillet; cook over medium heat about 8 minutes or until vegetables are tender. Stir in undrained tomatoes and, if desired, parsley. Bring to boiling; reduce heat. Simmer, uncovered, for 5 minutes.

4 Crumble bacon; stir bacon and tomato mixture into spaghetti mixture; heat through.

Nutrition Facts per serving: 178 cal., 2 g total fat (1 g sat. fat), 3 mg chol., 725 mg sodium, 35 g carbo., 7 g fiber, 9 g pro.
Daily Values: 105% vit. A, 25% vit. C, 7% calcium, 13% iron

Beet Borscht ♥

Depending on the variety of the beet, you may want to adjust the amount of sugar to taste. Favorite stir-ins for borscht are half-and-half, sour cream, and plain yogurt.

Prep: 20 minutes **Cook:** 30 minutes **Makes:** 4 servings (about 5 cups)

1½ pounds beets, tops
      removed
  2 small onions, halved
      lengthwise (about
      8 ounces)
  1 teaspoon salt
  5 cups water
  2 tablespoons sugar
  2 tablespoons lemon juice
 ¾ cup finely shredded green
      cabbage

1 Cut off beet roots and all but 1 inch of the stems; wash. Do not peel.

2 In a Dutch oven combine beets, onions, and salt. Add water. Bring to boiling; reduce heat. Simmer, covered, for 20 minutes. Cool slightly. Slip skins off beets; discard. Cut beets into large pieces.

3 Stir in sugar and lemon juice. Return to boiling; reduce heat. Simmer, uncovered, for 10 minutes. If desired, cover and chill.

4 To serve, ladle warm or cold soup into bowls, using one onion half per serving. Sprinkle cabbage over soup.

Nutrition Facts per serving: 107 cal., 0 g total fat (0 g sat. fat), 0 mg chol., 700 mg sodium, 25 g carbo., 5 g fiber, 3 g pro.
Daily Values: 5% vit. A, 34% vit. C, 7% calcium, 7% iron

Gingered Pumpkin-Pear Soup ♥ FAST

A swirl of lime-laced sour cream adds a burst of citrus flavor to this golden pumpkin soup. Serve it as a first course at a fall or winter dinner party.

Start to finish: 25 minutes **Makes:** 6 servings (about 6 cups)

½ cup chopped sweet onion
2 teaspoons grated fresh ginger
1 tablespoon butter
3 pears, peeled, cored, and sliced
1 15-ounce can pumpkin
1½ cups vegetable broth
1 cup milk
¼ cup light dairy sour cream
½ teaspoon finely shredded lime peel
1 tablespoon lime juice
Lime peel (optional)

1 In a large saucepan cook onion and ginger in hot butter over medium heat until onion is tender. Stir in pears; cook for 1 minute. Stir in pumpkin and broth. Bring to boiling; reduce heat. Simmer, covered, about 5 minutes more or until pears are tender. Cool slightly.

2 Place half of the pumpkin mixture in a blender container or food processor bowl. Cover and blend or process until smooth. Repeat with remaining pumpkin mixture. Return all of the mixture to saucepan; stir in milk. Heat through. Season to taste with salt and black pepper.

3 Meanwhile, stir together sour cream, the ½ teaspoon lime peel, and the lime juice. Drizzle some of the sour cream mixture over each serving. If desired, sprinkle with additional lime peel.

Nutrition Facts per serving: 129 cal., 4 g total fat (2 g sat. fat), 9 mg chol., 310 mg sodium, 24 g carbo., 5 g fiber, 3 g pro.
Daily Values: 162% vit. A, 13% vit. C, 7% calcium, 8% iron

Red Pepper Soup FAST

Herbes de Provence, a blend of herbs popular in southern France, lends a Mediterranean accent to this velvety smooth soup.

Start to finish: 30 minutes **Makes:** 4 servings (about 4 cups)

1 large red onion, coarsely chopped (1 cup)
3 cloves garlic
1 tablespoon butter
2 small red sweet peppers, coarsely chopped (1½ cups)
1 large tomato, chopped (¾ cup)
1 tablespoon ouzo or anise liqueur or ⅛ teaspoon anise seeds, crushed
½ teaspoon dried herbes de Provence or fines herbes, crushed
½ teaspoon paprika
1½ cups chicken broth
¼ cup dairy sour cream
1 recipe Lemon Sour Cream
Shredded lemon peel (optional)
Fresh tarragon sprigs (optional)

1 In a medium saucepan cook onion and garlic in hot butter over medium heat until tender. Add peppers; cover and cook for 8 to 10 minutes or until peppers are soft, stirring occasionally.

2 Add tomato, liqueur or anise seeds, herbes de Provence, and paprika. Add broth; bring to boiling. Remove from heat and cool slightly.

3 Place half of the pepper mixture in a blender container or food processor bowl. Cover and blend or process until smooth. Repeat with remaining mixture. Return all of the mixture to saucepan. Stir in the sour cream; heat through but do not boil.

4 To serve, ladle soup into bowls. Top each serving with about 1 tablespoon of the Lemon Sour Cream; draw a knife through the cream to swirl. If desired, garnish with lemon peel and tarragon sprigs.

Lemon Sour Cream: In a small bowl stir together ¼ cup dairy sour cream, ½ teaspoon finely shredded lemon peel, 1 teaspoon lemon juice, and a few drops bottled hot pepper sauce.

Nutrition Facts per serving: 150 cal., 10 g total fat (5 g sat. fat), 28 mg chol., 343 mg sodium, 11 g carbo., 1 g fiber, 4 g pro.
Daily Values: 53% vit. A, 127% vit. C

To Make Ahead: Prepare and blend soup as directed, but do not add sour cream. Transfer soup to a storage container. Cover and chill. Before serving, transfer soup to a saucepan; bring to boiling. Remove from heat; add the sour cream. Serve as directed.

Oysters Rockefeller Soup

Herbsaint, a liqueur made in New Orleans, contributes a distinctive anise flavor to this elegant soup modeled after the famous appetizer created in that city.

Prep: 35 minutes **Cook:** 30 minutes **Makes:** 12 servings (about 12½ cups)

5	stalks celery, finely chopped (2½ cups)
2	large onions, finely chopped (2 cups)
1	bay leaf
2	tablespoons butter
3	cups chopped fresh spinach
4	cups thinly sliced green onions
1¼	cups snipped fresh Italian flat-leaf parsley
1	clove garlic, minced
¼	teaspoon dried thyme, crushed
½	teaspoon dried oregano, crushed
2	teaspoons salt
⅛	teaspoon ground black pepper
⅛	teaspoon ground red pepper
⅛	teaspoon ground white pepper
1	tablespoon all-purpose flour
30	oysters (about 2 cups)
	Chicken broth or fish stock
¾	cup Herbsaint or Pernod
6	cups whipping cream
	Cracked red peppercorns (optional)

1 In a 4-quart Dutch oven or large saucepan cook celery, onions, and bay leaf in hot butter over medium-high heat for 4 to 5 minutes or until vegetables are tender. Reduce heat to low; add spinach, green onions, and parsley. Cook, stirring constantly, for 3 minutes. Remove bay leaf.

2 Add garlic, thyme, oregano, salt, and black, red, and white pepper. Cook, stirring constantly, for 4 minutes. Add flour and cook for 2 minutes, stirring constantly and scraping the sides and bottom of the pan.

3 Drain oysters, reserving liquid. If necessary, add enough broth to oyster liquid to make 1 cup total. Set aside.

4 Increase heat to medium-high and carefully add Herbsaint to spinach mixture. Cook, stirring constantly, for 4 to 5 minutes. Add oyster liquid and cook, stirring occasionally, for 4 minutes. Cool slightly.

5 Place spinach mixture in a blender container or food processor bowl. Cover and blend or process until smooth. Return all of the mixture to the pan. Stir in whipping cream. Cook over medium heat for 4 to 5 minutes or until heated through, stirring occasionally.

6 Add oysters and cook, stirring occasionally, about 5 minutes or until oyster edges curl. Serve immediately. If desired, sprinkle with cracked red peppercorns.

Nutrition Facts per serving: 538 cal., 47 g total fat (30 g sat. fat), 194 mg chol., 568 mg sodium, 18 g carbo., 2 g fiber, 7 g pro.
Daily Values: 77% vit. A, 39% vit. C, 12% calcium, 25% iron

Squash-Potato Chowder FAST

Liven up a can of cream of potato soup with fresh vegetables and herbs. This nifty soup fits the bill when you're planning a quick-to-fix soup and sandwich supper.

Prep: 10 minutes **Cook:** 20 minutes **Makes:** 6 servings (about 5¾ cups)

1 tablespoon butter
2 cups cubed summer
    squash, such as
    zucchini, sunburst,
    pattypan, or crookneck
1 cup sliced carrot
1 medium onion, chopped
    (½ cup)
1 clove garlic, minced
¾ teaspoon dried thyme,
    crushed
⅛ to ¼ teaspoon black
    pepper
1 10¾-ounce can condensed
    cream of potato soup
2 cups milk
   Fresh thyme sprigs or
    sliced green onions
    (optional)

1 In a large saucepan melt butter over medium-low heat. Add squash, carrot, onion, garlic, dried thyme, and pepper. Cover and cook for 15 to 20 minutes or until vegetables are crisp-tender, stirring occasionally.

2 Stir in soup and milk. Bring to boiling; reduce heat. Simmer, covered, for 5 minutes. Ladle soup into bowls. If desired, garnish with thyme sprigs.

Nutrition Facts per serving: 118 cal., 5 g total fat (3 g sat. fat), 14 mg chol., 476 mg sodium, 16 g carbo., 2 g fiber, 4 g pro.
Daily Values: 93% vit. A, 13% vit. C, 11% calcium, 5% iron

Baked Potato Soup

Speed preparation time by cooking the potatoes in your microwave oven. Garnish the finished soup with tasty baked potato toppers—cheese, green onion, and bacon.

Prep: 20 minutes **Bake:** 40 minutes **Cook:** 20 minutes **Makes:** 5 to 6 servings (about 5½ cups)

 2   large baking potatoes
       (about 8 ounces each)
 3   tablespoons thinly sliced
       green onion
 3   tablespoons butter
 3   tablespoons all-purpose
       flour
 2   teaspoons snipped fresh
       dill or chives or
       ¼ teaspoon dried
       dillweed
 ¼   teaspoon salt
 ¼   teaspoon black pepper
 4   cups milk
1¼   cups shredded American
       cheese (5 ounces)
 3   tablespoons thinly sliced
       green onion
 4   slices bacon, crisp-cooked,
       drained, and crumbled

1 Scrub potatoes thoroughly with a brush; pat dry. Prick potatoes with a fork. Bake in a 425° oven for 40 to 60 minutes or until tender. Let cool. Cut potatoes in half lengthwise; gently scoop out potato pulp. Break up any large pieces of potato. Discard potato skins.

2 In a large saucepan cook 3 tablespoons green onion in hot butter over medium heat until tender. Stir in flour, dill, salt, and pepper. Add milk all at once. Cook and stir for 12 to 15 minutes or until thickened and bubbly. Add the potato pulp and 1 cup of the cheese; stir until cheese melts.

3 To serve, ladle soup into bowls. Top with the remaining cheese, 3 tablespoons green onion, and bacon.

Nutrition Facts per serving: 377 cal., 23 g total fat (14 g sat. fat), 67 mg chol., 801 mg sodium, 26 g carbo., 1 g fiber, 17 g pro.
Daily Values: 21% vit. A, 23% vit. C, 43% calcium, 7% iron

Chilled Carrot Bisque

This sweet, creamy, and vitamin-rich soup makes a good addition to a meatless menu. The soup gets added protein from split peas, but your family will never guess they're there.

Prep: 1 hour **Chill:** 4 hours **Makes:** 4 servings (about 4 cups)

Nonstick cooking spray
¼ cup chopped red onion
1 large clove garlic, minced
4 medium carrots, sliced
(about 2 cups)
½ cup dry yellow split peas,
rinsed and drained
3½ cups chicken broth or two
14-ounce cans reduced-
sodium chicken broth
2 teaspoons finely shredded
orange peel
½ cup orange juice
2 teaspoons brown sugar
⅛ teaspoon ground nutmeg
Dash ground red pepper
½ cup fat-free sour cream
2 tablespoons fat-free milk
(optional)
Snipped fresh chives

1 Lightly coat a large saucepan with cooking spray. Add onion, garlic, and carrots. Cook and stir over medium heat for 3 to 5 minutes or until onion is tender. Add split peas, broth, and orange peel. Bring to boiling; reduce heat. Simmer, covered, about 45 minutes or until carrots and peas are very tender.

2 Place half of the carrot mixture in a blender container or food processor bowl. Cover and blend or process until smooth. Repeat with remaining mixture. Return all of the carrot mixture to the saucepan.

3 Stir in orange juice, brown sugar, nutmeg, and ground red pepper. Cook and stir over low heat about 5 minutes or just until sugar has dissolved and flavors blend. Remove from heat and cool slightly. Pour soup into a medium bowl; cover and chill at least 4 hours.

4 To serve, add salt, brown sugar, or ground red pepper to taste. Stir sour cream until smooth, adding 2 tablespoons fat-free milk, if necessary; gently swirl it into soup. Sprinkle with chives. Serve cold.

Nutrition Facts per serving: 197 cal., 2 g total fat (0 g sat. fat), 0 mg chol., 631 mg sodium, 34 g carbo., 4 g fiber, 11 g pro.
Daily Values: 165% vit. A, 33% vit. C, 11% iron

To Make Ahead: Prepare soup as directed. Refrigerate up to 2 days.

Sweet Potato and Pear Vichyssoise

Sweet potatoes and pears replace the standard white potatoes in this French classic. Like the original, the soup can be sipped hot or cold.

Prep: 20 minutes **Cook:** 30 minutes **Makes:** 6 servings (about 5 cups)

⅔ cup sliced leeks (about 2 medium)
1 tablespoon butter
2 cups cubed, peeled sweet potatoes (about 2 medium)
1 14-ounce can chicken broth
¾ cup chopped, peeled pear (1 medium)
1 teaspoon snipped fresh thyme or ¼ teaspoon dried thyme, crushed
⅛ teaspoon salt
⅛ teaspoon black pepper
1 cup half-and-half or light cream
Fresh thyme sprigs (optional)
Pear slices (optional)

1 In a saucepan cook and stir leeks in hot butter over medium heat until tender. Stir in sweet potatoes, broth, chopped pear, snipped thyme, salt, and pepper. Bring to boiling; reduce heat. Simmer, covered, for 25 to 35 minutes or until potatoes are very tender. Cool slightly.

2 Place half of the sweet potato mixture in a blender container or food processor bowl. Cover and blend or process until smooth; transfer to a bowl. Repeat with remaining mixture. Stir half-and-half into the sweet potato mixture.

3 If serving warm, return vichyssoise to saucepan; heat through. Serve immediately. If serving chilled, place mixture in a covered container; chill for 4 to 24 hours. If desired, garnish with thyme sprigs and pear slices.

Nutrition Facts per serving: 151 cal., 7 g total fat (4 g sat. fat), 20 mg chol., 309 mg sodium, 19 g carbo., 4 g fiber, 4 g pro.
Daily Values: 96% vit. A, 22% vit. C, 6% calcium, 6% iron

Leek-Gruyère Cream Soup

The subtle onion flavor of leeks blends sumptuously with the rich, nutty taste of Gruyère cheese in this satiny smooth soup. Be sure to use fresh-looking leeks with crisp green leaves.

Prep: 20 minutes. **Cook:** 15 minutes. **Makes:** 8 servings (about 7½ cups)

6 cups chicken broth
4 cups sliced leeks
1 cup sliced fresh
    mushrooms
1 teaspoon dried fines
    herbes, crushed
½ teaspoon white pepper
⅓ cup all-purpose flour
1½ cups shredded process
    Gruyère cheese
    (6 ounces)
2 tablespoons snipped fresh
    parsley
1 cup whipping cream
    Thinly sliced leeks
    (optional)

1 In a Dutch oven combine 4 cups of the broth, the 4 cups leeks, mushrooms, fines herbes, and pepper. Bring to boiling; reduce heat. Simmer, covered, for 10 to 15 minutes or until leeks are tender. Cool slightly.

2 Place one-third of the leek mixture in a blender container or food processor bowl. Cover and blend or process until smooth. Repeat twice with remaining leek mixture. Return all of the leek mixture to pan. Stir in 1 cup of the remaining broth.

3 In a small bowl stir together the remaining 1 cup of broth and the flour until smooth. Stir into leek mixture in Dutch oven. Stir in cheese and parsley. Cook and stir over medium-low heat until slightly thickened and bubbly and cheese melts. Stir in whipping cream; heat through but do not boil. If desired, garnish with additional sliced leeks.

Nutrition Facts per serving: 257 cal., 19 g total fat (11 g sat. fat), 60 mg chol., 768 mg sodium, 12 g carbo., 1 g fiber, 10 g pro.
Daily Values: 11% vit. A, 10% vit. C, 21% calcium, 10% iron

Iced Yellow Tomato Soup

You can make this recipe with ripe red tomatoes too. For a vegetarian version, substitute an equal amount of vegetable broth for the chicken broth.

Prep: 15 minutes **Chill:** 4 hours **Makes:** 8 servings (about 6 cups)

2 14-ounce cans reduced-sodium chicken broth

1½ pounds yellow tomatoes, peeled, seeded, and cut up (about 5 medium)

1 large yellow sweet pepper

2 to 3 yellow banana peppers, seeded and chopped

4 cloves garlic, chopped

½ small onion

1 small roma tomato, peeled, seeded, and diced

Fresh whole chives (optional)

1 In a blender container or food processor bowl combine half of the broth, half of the yellow tomatoes, half of the sweet pepper, half of the banana peppers, half of the garlic, and half of the onion. Cover and blend or process until smooth. Repeat.

2 Transfer soup to bowl. Cover and chill for 4 to 24 hours. To serve, ladle soup into chilled bowls. Top with diced roma tomato and, if desired, garnish with fresh whole chives.

Nutrition Facts per serving: 41 cal., 1 g total fat (0 g sat. fat), 0 mg chol., 299 mg sodium, 7 g carbo., 1 g fiber, 2 g pro.
Daily Values: 7% vit. A, 107% vit. C, 3% iron

Farmer's Vegetable Broth ♥

Many different root vegetables will work in this versatile home-style soup. Try an equal amount of potato or fennel in place of one of the vegetables listed.

Start to finish: 45 minutes **Makes:** 4 to 6 servings (about 8 cups)

2 medium leeks, trimmed and bias-cut into 1- to 2-inch slices

1 medium rutabaga, peeled and cut into 1-inch pieces

1 medium turnip, peeled and cut into 1-inch pieces

1 small parsnip, peeled and cut up

1 small carrot, peeled and cut up

3 cups beef broth

3 cups water

½ cup dry sherry or beef broth

1 4-inch sprig fresh rosemary or ½ teaspoon dried rosemary, crushed

1 In a Dutch oven combine leeks, rutabaga, turnip, parsnip, carrot, broth, water, sherry, and rosemary. Bring to boiling; reduce heat. Simmer, uncovered, for 25 to 30 minutes or until turnip and rutabaga are tender. Discard rosemary sprig (if using).

2 To serve, ladle into bowls. If desired, garnish with additional rosemary sprigs.

Nutrition Facts per serving: 123 cal., 0 g total fat (0 g sat. fat), 0 mg chol., 678 mg sodium, 18 g carbo., 4 g fiber, 3 g pro.
Daily Values: 28% vit. A, 42% vit. C, 7% calcium, 7% iron

Fresh Mushroom Soup FAST

Revive the tradition of making homemade soup with fresh mushrooms. This one uses oyster mushrooms and your choice of shiitake or white button mushrooms.

Prep: 10 minutes **Cook:** 10 minutes **Makes:** 6 servings (about 4¾ cups)

8 ounces shiitake or button mushrooms
6 ounces small oyster mushrooms
⅓ cup chopped shallots
2 tablespoons butter
2 tablespoons all-purpose flour
½ teaspoon salt
¼ teaspoon coarsely ground black pepper
1 14-ounce can vegetable broth or chicken broth (1¾ cups)
2 cups half-and-half or light cream
⅛ teaspoon ground saffron or saffron threads
Saffron threads (optional)

1 Remove any tough or woody stems from the mushrooms. Cut large shiitake mushrooms in half. Chop the remaining shiitake mushrooms. Cut oyster mushrooms into large pieces.

2 In a large saucepan cook all of the mushrooms and shallots in hot butter over medium-high heat for 4 to 5 minutes or until tender, stirring occasionally.

3 Stir in flour, salt, and pepper. Add broth. Cook and stir over medium heat until slightly thickened and bubbly. Cook and stir for 1 minute more. Stir in half-and-half and saffron; heat through. To serve, ladle soup into bowls. If desired, top with saffron threads.

Nutrition Facts per serving: 193 cal., 14 g total fat (8 g sat. fat), 40 mg chol., 565 mg sodium, 15 g carbo., 2 g fiber, 5 g pro.
Daily Values: 15% vit. A, 3% vit. C, 9% calcium, 5% iron

To Make Ahead: Prepare soup as directed. Cool soup. Transfer to an airtight container. Store in the refrigerator up to 2 days or seal, label, and freeze up to 3 months. To reheat, transfer frozen soup to a large saucepan. Cook, covered, over medium heat until heated through, stirring occasionally.

Alpine Cheese Soup

Rolled oats give this cream soup extra body. Leeks, Gruyère cheese, and a sprinkle of bacon ensure a rich and savory flavor.

Prep: 25 minutes **Cook:** 25 minutes **Makes:** 6 servings (about 5 cups)

4 slices bacon
1 medium onion, chopped (½ cup)
1 stalk celery, chopped
1 medium leek (white part only), halved lengthwise and sliced (⅓ cup)
2 14-ounce cans reduced-sodium chicken broth
½ cup quick-cooking rolled oats
¼ teaspoon black pepper
¾ cup shredded process Gruyère or Swiss cheese (3 ounces)
¼ cup whipping cream, half-and-half, or light cream
2 tablespoons snipped fresh parsley

1 In a large saucepan cook bacon over medium heat until crisp. Drain bacon on paper towels, reserving drippings in saucepan. Crumble bacon; set aside.

2 Cook onion, celery, and leek in the reserved bacon drippings over medium heat about 5 minutes or until tender. Stir in broth, oats, and pepper. Bring to boiling; reduce heat. Simmer, covered, for 20 minutes. Remove from heat. Stir in shredded cheese. Cool slightly.

3 Place half of the soup in a blender container or food processor bowl. Cover and blend or process until smooth. Repeat with remaining soup. Return all of the soup to saucepan; stir in cream. Heat through but do not boil. Ladle into bowls; sprinkle with crumbled bacon and snipped parsley.

Nutrition Facts per serving: 161 cal., 11 g total fat (6 g sat. fat), 33 mg chol., 442 mg sodium, 8 g carbo., 1 g fiber, 9 g pro.
Daily Values: 8% vit. A, 7% vit. C, 17% calcium, 6% iron

Cumin Butternut Squash Soup

Slices of intensely colored blood oranges make a pleasing garnish for this velvety soup. If blood oranges aren't available, choose another variety of orange with a thin skin.

Prep: 30 minutes   **Cook:** 20 minutes   **Makes:** 8 servings (about 7 cups)

1 to 2 teaspoons cumin
   seeds
¼ cup butter
1 medium onion, chopped
   (½ cup)
½ cup chopped carrot
½ cup chopped celery
2 pounds butternut squash,
   peeled and coarsely
   chopped (5 cups)
1 teaspoon ground cumin
3 cups reduced-sodium
   chicken broth
1⅓ cups buttermilk
½ teaspoon salt
⅛ teaspoon black pepper
   Blood oranges or oranges,
   thinly sliced (optional)

1 In a small skillet cook cumin seeds over medium heat about 1 minute or until seeds become fragrant and turn a shade darker, stirring frequently. Immediately remove seeds from skillet; set aside.

2 In a large saucepan melt butter. Stir in onion, carrot, and celery. Cook over medium heat for 5 minutes, stirring occasionally. Stir in squash and ground cumin. Cook and stir for 5 minutes more. Add broth. Bring to boiling; reduce heat. Simmer, covered, about 8 to 10 minutes or until vegetables are very tender. Cool slightly.

3 Place one-fourth of the squash mixture in a blender container or food processor bowl. Cover and blend or process until smooth. Repeat with remaining squash mixture. Return all of the mixture to the pan. Stir in buttermilk, salt, and pepper; heat through. To serve, ladle into bowls. If desired, top with orange slices. Sprinkle with toasted cumin seeds.

Nutrition Facts per serving: 125 cal., 7 g total fat (4 g sat. fat), 18 mg chol., 497 mg sodium, 15 g carbo., 2 g fiber, 4 g pro.
Daily Values: 180% vit. A, 34% vit. C, 10% calcium, 5% iron

Gazpacho To Go

Keep this easy-to-tote soup in mind for summertime picnics or potlucks. Show off the mosaic of colors by carrying it in a clear plastic storage container; transport it in an ice-filled cooler.

Prep: 30 minutes **Chill:** 2 to 24 hours **Makes:** 6 servings (about 7 cups)

1   15-ounce can chunky Italian- or salsa-style tomatoes, undrained

2   cups quartered yellow pear-shaped tomatoes and/or halved cherry tomatoes

1   15-ounce can garbanzo beans (chickpeas), rinsed and drained

1¼ cups hot-style vegetable juice or vegetable juice

1   cup beef broth

½   cup coarsely chopped, seeded cucumber

½   cup coarsely chopped yellow and/or red sweet pepper

¼   cup coarsely chopped red onion

¼   cup snipped fresh cilantro

3   tablespoons lime juice or lemon juice

2   cloves garlic, minced

¼ to ½ teaspoon bottled hot pepper sauce

1 In a large bowl combine canned and fresh tomatoes, garbanzo beans, vegetable juice, broth, cucumber, sweet pepper, onion, cilantro, lime juice, garlic, and hot pepper sauce. Cover and chill for 2 to 24 hours.

2 To serve, ladle soup into bowls or mugs.

Nutrition Facts per serving: 142 cal., 5 g total fat (0 g sat. fat), 0 mg chol., 1,145 mg sodium, 27 g carbo., 5 g fiber, 7 g pro.
Daily Values: 33% vit. A, 131% vit. C, 5% calcium, 24% iron

Fresh Pea Soup FAST

Mild Boston lettuce mellows the flavor of garden-fresh peas in this exquisite soup. You can make the chilled soup up to one day ahead for an easy-to-serve first course.

Prep: 20 minutes **Cook:** 10 minutes **Makes:** 4 to 6 servings (about 5 cups)

3 cups water
2 cups shelled fresh peas or one 10-ounce package frozen peas
1 small onion, chopped (⅓ cup)
2 tablespoons snipped fresh parsley
½ teaspoon salt
2 tablespoons butter
2 cups torn Boston lettuce
¼ cup milk or half-and-half
¼ cup vermouth (optional)
  Dairy sour cream (optional)
  Fresh parsley sprigs (optional)

1 In a large saucepan combine water, peas, onion, snipped parsley, and salt. Bring to boiling; reduce heat. Simmer, covered, for 10 to 12 minutes or until peas are tender.

2 Meanwhile, melt butter in a skillet. Add lettuce and cook just until soft. Add the lettuce mixture to the pea mixture.

3 Place half of the pea mixture in a blender container or food processor bowl. Cover and blend or process until smooth. Repeat with remaining mixture. Return all of the mixture to the saucepan. Add milk and, if desired, vermouth. Heat through. Season to taste with salt and black pepper. Transfer mixture to a bowl. Cover and chill for 2 to 24 hours. To serve, ladle soup into chilled bowls. If desired, top with sour cream and parsley sprigs.

Nutrition Facts per serving: 123 cal., 6 g total fat (4 g sat. fat), 16 mg chol., 338 mg sodium, 13 g carbo., 3 g fiber, 5 g pro.
Daily Values: 12% vit. A, 23% vit. C

Carrot and Chile Pepper Soup

FAST

Include this soup in a Mexican or Tex-Mex meal along with fajitas or burritos. Use hot, medium, or mild chiles to suit your taste and the rest of the meal.

Start to finish: 30 minutes **Makes:** 8 servings (about 7 cups)

2 14-ounce cans vegetable broth

16 ounces packaged peeled baby carrots

1 large onion, chopped (1 cup)

1 4-ounce can diced green chile peppers, undrained

1 teaspoon chili powder

½ teaspoon ground cumin

1 cup light cream or half-and-half

Fresh purple basil leaves (optional)

1 In a large saucepan or Dutch oven combine broth, carrots, onion, undrained chile peppers, chili powder, and cumin. Bring to boiling; reduce heat. Simmer, covered, about 12 minutes or until carrots are very tender.

2 Place half of the mixture in a blender container or food processor bowl. Cover and blend or process until smooth. Repeat with remaining mixture. Return all of the mixture to saucepan. Stir in light cream; heat through. Ladle soup into bowls. If desired, garnish with purple basil.

Nutrition Facts per serving: 75 cal., 4 g total fat (2 g sat. fat), 11 mg chol., 510 mg sodium, 10 g carbo., 2 g fiber, 2 g pro.
Daily Values: 133% vit. A, 11% vit. C, 6% calcium, 5% iron

Baby Vegetable Minestrone ♥

Baby vegetables possess a milder flavor and a more tender texture than their full-size counterparts. Be sure to cook them just until tender for optimal taste and texture in this eye-appealing soup.

Prep: 20 minutes **Cook:** 25 minutes **Makes:** 6 servings (about 7½ cups)

2 teaspoons olive oil
1 bulb baby fennel, thinly sliced
1 medium carrot, peeled and finely diced or chopped
2 large cloves garlic, minced
¼ teaspoon lemon-pepper seasoning
2 14-ounce cans reduced-sodium chicken broth
½ cup dried ditalini or other small dried pasta
6 ounces baby zucchini, halved lengthwise (about 1 dozen)
6 ounces baby yellow squash, halved lengthwise (about 1 dozen)
½ cup sliced green onions
¼ cup fresh basil leaves, thinly sliced
6 ounces dried aged cheese, such as Parmigiano-Reggiano, Romano, or Padano, cut into six very thin wedges (optional)

1 Heat oil in a 4-quart saucepan over medium heat. Add fennel, carrot, garlic, and lemon-pepper seasoning. Cook and stir for 3 to 4 minutes or until carrot is slightly browned. Carefully stir in broth. Bring to boiling; reduce heat. Simmer, covered, about 8 minutes or just until vegetables are tender.

2 Add pasta. Simmer, covered, for 5 minutes. Add zucchini and squash. Return to boiling; reduce heat. Simmer, covered, for 5 minutes more or until pasta is tender. Stir in the green onions and basil.

3 If desired, place a wedge of cheese in each of 6 bowls. Add the hot soup. Let cheese soften slightly before serving.

Nutrition Facts per serving: 83 cal., 2 g total fat (0 g sat. fat), 0 mg chol., 410 mg sodium, 13 g carbo., 4 g fiber, 4 g pro.
Daily Values: 29% vit. A, 14% vit. C, 3% calcium, 5% iron

German Potato Soup

Bacon, caraway seeds, and the tang of sour cream give this hot soup a flavor reminiscent of German potato salad. Serve with a platter of sliced cheese, deli meats, and rye bread.

Start to finish: 40 minutes **Makes:** 6 servings (about 7 cups)

 4 slices bacon
 2 medium carrots, chopped
       (1 cup)
 1 medium leek (white part
       only), chopped (⅓ cup)
 1 medium onion, chopped
       (½ cup)
 4 cups beef broth
 1 pound potatoes
       (3 medium), coarsely
       chopped (about 3 cups)
 1 cup chopped cabbage
 ¼ cup chopped fresh parsley
 1 bay leaf
 ½ to 1 teaspoon black
       pepper
 ½ teaspoon caraway seeds
 ¼ teaspoon ground nutmeg
 ½ cup dairy sour cream

1 In a 4- or 4½-quart Dutch oven cook bacon over medium heat until crisp. Drain bacon on paper towels, reserving 2 tablespoons drippings in Dutch oven. Crumble bacon; set aside.

2 Cook carrots, leek, and onion in reserved drippings in Dutch oven until nearly tender. Stir in broth. Bring to boiling. Stir in potatoes, cabbage, parsley, bay leaf, pepper, caraway seeds, and nutmeg. Return to boiling; reduce heat. Simmer, covered, for 12 to 15 minutes or until potatoes are tender. Discard bay leaf.

3 Place sour cream in a small bowl. Gradually whisk about 1 cup of the hot liquid into sour cream; whisk sour cream mixture into the soup mixture. Stir in bacon. Heat through but do not boil.

Nutrition Facts per serving: 188 cal., 11 g total fat (5 g sat. fat), 15 mg chol., 636 mg sodium, 18 g carbo., 3 g fiber, 6 g pro.
Daily Values: 108% vit. A, 33% vit. C, 5% calcium, 8% iron

Strawberry-Melon Soup

This tangy soup is the perfect way to start a spring or summer brunch. If using the flower garnish, be sure to use petals from plants that have been grown without pesticides.

Prep: 30 minute. **Cook:** 5 minutes **Chill:** 8 hours **Makes:** 8 to 10 servings (about 8 cups)

1   small cantaloupe
½   of a small honeydew melon
½   cup unsweetened pineapple juice
⅓   cup sugar
1   tablespoon grated fresh ginger
4   cups fresh or frozen unsweetened strawberries
1   8-ounce carton vanilla yogurt
1   8-ounce carton dairy sour cream
2   cups milk
     Edible carnation petals (optional)

1 Using a small melon baller, scoop the cantaloupe and the honeydew into balls, or use a knife to cut melons into cubes. (You should have about 4 cups cantaloupe and 2 cups honeydew.) Set melon aside.

2 In a small saucepan combine pineapple juice, sugar, and ginger. Bring to boiling, stirring until sugar dissolves; reduce heat. Simmer, uncovered, over medium heat for 5 to 7 minutes or until the mixture is the consistency of a thin syrup. Remove from heat; cool. Transfer syrup to a storage container. Add 2 cups of the cantaloupe pieces and all of the honeydew pieces. Cover and chill overnight.

3 Meanwhile, in a blender container or food processor bowl cover and blend or process strawberries until smooth; remove and set aside. Cover and blend or process remaining 2 cups cantaloupe pieces until smooth. In a large mixing bowl stir together yogurt and sour cream. Add pureed strawberries, pureed melon, and milk; stir until combined. Cover and chill overnight.

4 To serve, drain melon balls, reserving syrup. Stir reserved syrup into the chilled soup. Ladle soup into chilled bowls; top with melon balls. If desired, garnish with carnation petals.

Nutrition Facts per serving: 220 cal., 8 g total fat (5 g sat. fat), 19 mg chol., 77 mg sodium, 34 g carbo., 3 g fiber, 6 g pro.
Daily Values: 60% vit. A, 147% vit. C, 18% calcium, 3% iron

Chilled Peach-Yogurt Soup

Begin or end your meal with this refreshingly cool soup. Serve it as a first course or as a fruity low-calorie dessert.

Prep: 15 minutes **Chill:** 2 to 24 hours **Makes:** 4 servings (about 2½ cups)

2 cups sliced, peeled peaches or frozen unsweetened peach slices
¾ cup peach or apricot nectar
¼ teaspoon ground cinnamon
1 8-ounce carton vanilla yogurt
Fresh mint sprigs (optional)
Raspberries (optional)

1 Thaw peaches, if frozen; do not drain. Place peach slices, nectar, and cinnamon in a blender container or food processor bowl. Cover and blend or process until smooth.

2 If desired, reserve 2 tablespoons of the yogurt for garnish. Place remaining yogurt in a large bowl. Add a little of the peach mixture to the remaining yogurt, stirring until smooth. Stir in the remaining peach mixture. Cover and chill for 2 to 24 hours.

3 To serve, ladle soup into chilled bowls. If desired, garnish with the reserved yogurt, fresh mint, and raspberries.

Nutrition Facts per serving: 113 cal., 1 g total fat (0 g sat. fat), 3 mg chol., 37 mg sodium, 24 g carbo., 2 g fiber, 3 g pro.
Daily Values: 10% vit. A, 20% vit. C, 10% calcium, 1% iron

Tutti-Frutti Spiced Fruit Soup FAST

Make up your own dried fruit mix to suit your preference. Want something a little stronger? Stir in a splash of brandy or rum before serving.

Start to finish: 25 minutes **Makes:** 8 servings (about 6 cups)

4 cups apple cider or apple juice

1½ cups apricot nectar

4 cranberry-flavored tea bags

7 ounces mixed dried fruits, such as apples, pears, apricots, plums, and/or persimmons

3 medium cooking apples (such as Granny Smith, Jonathan, or Braeburn), cored and cut into large chunks

1 In a saucepan combine apple cider and apricot nectar. Bring to boiling; remove from heat. Add tea bags. Steep for 3 minutes. Remove tea bags; discard.

2 Meanwhile, cut up any large pieces of dried fruit. Add dried fruit and apple chunks to saucepan. Return to boiling; reduce heat. Simmer, uncovered, about 5 minutes or just until fresh apple chunks are cooked and dried fruit is tender. (Don't overcook the fresh apples.) To serve, ladle the fruit and liquid into bowls.

Nutrition Facts per serving: 165 cal., 0 g total fat (0 g sat. fat), 0 mg chol., 6 mg sodium, 32 g carbo., 2 g fiber, 1 g pro.
Daily Values: 12% vit. A, 7% vit. C, 2% calcium, 8% iron

Farmer's Market Melon Soup

For the smoothest texture and richest flavor, use only ripe melons in this ginger-scented soup. This tantalizing soup makes a lovely brunch or luncheon dish.

Prep: 20 minutes **Chill:** 2 to 24 hours **Makes:** 8 servings (about 6 cups)

1 medium golden honeydew melon, Persian melon, or cantaloupe, peeled, seeded, and cut up (about 6 cups)
¾ cup apricot nectar
¾ cup plain nonfat yogurt
1 tablespoon grated fresh ginger
2 fresh red and/or green serrano peppers, bias-sliced very thin (see tip, page 12) (optional)

1 In a blender container or food processor bowl combine half of the melon, half of the apricot nectar, half of the yogurt, and half of the ginger. Cover and blend or process until smooth. Transfer to a large bowl. Repeat with remaining melon, nectar, yogurt, and ginger. Stir into mixture in bowl.

2 Cover and chill for 2 to 24 hours. To serve, ladle the soup into chilled bowls. If desired, garnish each serving with several pepper slices.

Nutrition Facts per serving: 69 cal., 1 g total fat (0 g sat. fat), 1 mg chol., 27 mg sodium, 15 g carbo., 1 g fiber, 2 g pro.
Daily Values: 42% vit. A, 97% vit. C, 4% calcium, 2% iron

INDEX

Photographs indicated in **bold**.

A-B

African Chicken Stew, 46
Alpine Cheese Soup, 176
Asian Chicken Noodle
  Soup, **14, 15**
Asian Turkey and Rice Soup, 22
Asparagus
  Lemon and Scallop Soup, **97**
  Springtime Soup, **121**
  Spring Vegetable Soup, **139**
A to Z Vegetable Soup, 126, **127**
Baby Vegetable Minestrone, 181
Baked Potato Soup, 168
Beans
  A to Z Vegetable
    Soup, 126, **127**
  Bean and Brussels Sprouts
    Stew, **154, 155**
  Beef and Red Bean
    Chili, 58, **59**
  Cassoulet-Style Stew, 84
  Chicken and Vegetable Bean
    Soup, 13
  Chicken Chili with
    Rice, 36, **37**
  Chili Blanco, 38
  Chili with Cornmeal
    Dumplings, 57
  Country Fish Stew, 118
  Endive, Ham, and Bean
    Soup, 70
  Garbanzo Bean Stew, 152
  Gazpacho To Go, 178
  Gingersnap Stew, 79
  Greek Minestrone, **119, 131**
  Hearty Turkey Soup, 11
  Italian Bean Soup, 122
  Italian Chili, 60
  Meatball Soup, **50**
  Minestrone, 161
  Moroccan Chicken
    Stew, **42,** 43
  Pasta and Bean Chicken
    Soup, 28
  Root Vegetable and Bean Soup,
    137
  Salsa Verde Beef Stew, **61**

Southwestern Bean and
  Chicken Soup, 25
Tex-Mex Chili, 56
Two-Bean Chili, 150
Vegetable Chili with
  Cheese, **149**
Veggie Soup with Curry
  Croutons, **144,** 145
White Bean and Cumin Chili,
  151
White Chili in a Bread
  Bowl, **39**
Winter Vegetable Soup, 135
Beef
  Beef and Red Bean
    Chili, 58, **59**
  Beef Broth, 48
  Beef Ragout, **86**
  Beef Stew with Lentils, 64
  Beefy Vegetable Soup, **49**
  Carbonnade of Beef and
    Vegetables, 65
  Chili with Cornmeal
    Dumplings, 57
  Chinese Beef and Noodle
    Soup, 51
  Green Chile Stew, **62**
  Hamburger Soup, 54
  Italian Beef Soup, **55**
  Italian Chili, 60
  Italian Wedding Soup, 52, **53**
  Meatball Soup, **50**
  Old-Time Beef Stew, 63
  Salsa Verde Beef Stew, **61**
Beet Borscht, 162, **163**
Beet Soup, Potato-, **142**
Biscuits, Green Onion, 30
Bouillabaisse, Moroccan, 117
Bratwurst and Potato Soup, 71
Broccoli-Chicken Soup,
  Creamy, **31**
Broth and stock
  Beef Broth, 48
  Chicken Broth, 8
  Fish Stock, 88
  Vegetable Broth, 120
Brunswick Stew, 41
Brussels Sprouts Stew, Bean
  and, **154,** 155

C-D

Cabbage
  Country Fish Stew, 118
  Italian Lentil Soup, **128**
Cajun Fish Soup, 89
Caramelized Onion
  Soup, 132, **133**
Carbonnade of Beef and
  Vegetables, 65
Caribbean Seafood
  Stew, 112, **113**
Carolina Catfish Stew, 114
Carrots
  Carrot and Chile Pepper
    Soup, **180**
  Chilled Carrot Bisque, 169
Cassoulet-Style Stew, 84
Catalan Chicken Chowder, **7, 34**
Cauliflower Chowder, Cheesy, 147
Cheese
  Alpine Cheese Soup, 176
  Cheese Toasts, 99
  Cheesy Cauliflower
    Chowder, 147
  Cheesy Cornmeal
    Dumplings, 57
  Corn and Cheese
    Chowder, 148
  Leek-Gruyère Cream
    Soup, **171**
  Vegetable Chili with
    Cheese, **149**
  Wild Rice and Cheese
    Soup, 129
Chicken
  African Chicken Stew, 46
  Asian Chicken Noodle
    Soup, **14, 15**
  Brunswick Stew, 41
  Catalan Chicken
    Chowder, **7, 34**
  Chicken and Vegetable Bean
    Soup, 13
  Chicken and Wild Rice
    Soup, 29
  Chicken Broth, 8
  Chicken Chili with Rice, 36, **37**
  Chicken 'n' Dumpling
    Soup, 10
  Chicken Soup with
    Cavatappi, 23

Chicken Stew with
  Tortellini, 45
Chicken Tortilla Soup, 27
Chicken Vegetable Ragout, 44
Chipotle Chicken Soup, 17
Classic Chicken-Sausage
  Gumbo, **40**
Creamy Broccoli-Chicken
  Soup, **31**
Creamy Chicken-Vegetable
  Soup, 18
Easy Mulligatawny Soup, **19**
Fennel-Potato Soup, **26**
Garden Chicken Soup, **9**
Indian Chicken Soup, 12
Mexican Chicken Posole, **21**
Moroccan Chicken
  Stew, **42, **43
Pasta and Bean Chicken
  Soup, 28
Ranch Chicken Chowder, 33
Southwestern Bean and
  Chicken Soup, 25
Thai Chicken-Coconut
  Soup, 16
White Chili in a Bread
  Bowl, **39**

Chili
Beef and Red Bean Chili, 58,
  59
Chicken Chili with Rice, 36, **37**
Chili Blanco, 38
Chili with Cornmeal
  Dumplings, 57
Italian Chili, 60
Tex-Mex Chili, 56
Two-Bean Chili, 150
Vegetable Chili with
  Cheese, **149**
White Bean and Cumin
  Chili, **151**
White Chili in a Bread
  Bowl, **39**
Chilled Carrot Bisque, 169
Chilled Peach Yogurt Soup, **184**
Chinese Beef and Noodle
  Soup, 51
Chipotle Chicken Soup, **17**

Chowder
Catalan Chicken
  Chowder, **7, **34
Cheesy Cauliflower
  Chowder, **147**
Chunky Ham and Potato
  Chowder, 75
Corn and Cheese Chowder,
  148
Corny Sausage
  Chowder, **76, **77
Easy Turkey Chowder, 32
Effortless Shrimp Chowder,
  109
Maryland Crab and Corn
  Chowder, 108
North Sea Chowder, 105
Ranch Chicken Chowder, 33
Red Seafood Chowder, **106**
Salmon Confetti Chowder, 110
Salmon Pan Chowder, 107
Spicy Corn Chowder, **104**
Squash-Potato Chowder, **167**
Turkey and Sweet Potato
  Chowder, 35
Chunky Ham and Potato
  Chowder, 75
Chunky Ratatouille Stew, 156
Chunky Vegetable-Cod Soup, 93
Classic Chicken-Sausage
  Gumbo, 40

Corn
Corn and Cheese Chowder,
  148
Corny Sausage
  Chowder, **76, **77
Garbanzo Bean Stew, 152
Maryland Crab and Corn
  Chowder, 108
Roasted Corn and Crab
  Soup, 96
Spicy Corn Chowder, **104**
Country Fish Stew, 118

Crab
Maryland Crab and Corn
  Chowder, 108
Roasted Corn and Crab
  Soup, 96
Spicy Corn Chowder, **104**
Cracker Mix, 99

Cream of Roasted Fennel
  Soup, **160**
Creamy Broccoli-Chicken
  Soup, **31**
Creamy Chicken-Vegetable
  Soup, 18
Creamy Ham and Vegetable
  Stew, 78
Creamy Shrimp and Spinach
  Stew, **111**

Croutons
Curry Croutons, 145
Herbed Croutons, 99
Rye Croutons, 26
Cumin Butternut Squash
  Soup, **177**
Curried Pumpkin Soup, 67
Curried Split Pea Soup, **72**
Curry Croutons, 145
Dumplings for Stew, 99

E-F

Easy Mulligatawny Soup, **19**
Easy Squash Soup, **159**
Easy Turkey Chowder, 32
Effortless Shrimp Chowder, 109
Emerald Soup, 141
Endive, Ham, and Bean Soup, 70
Farmer's Market Melon
  Soup, **186**
Farmer's Vegetable
  Broth, **157, 173**

Fennel
Bean and Brussels Sprouts
  Stew, **154, **155
Cream of Roasted Fennel
  Soup, **160**
Fennel-Potato Soup, **26**
Fish and shellfish. *See also* Crab,
Oysters, Salmon, Scallops, Shrimp
Cajun Fish Soup, 89
Caribbean Seafood
  Stew, 112, **113**
Carolina Catfish Stew, 114
Chunky Vegetable-Cod
  Soup, 93
Country Fish Stew, 118
Fish Soup Provençale, **90**
Fish Stock, 88
Italian Fish and Vegetable
  Soup, 91

Moroccan Bouillabaisse, 117
North Sea Chowder, 105
Red Pepper and Snapper
    Soup, **87, 92**
Red Seafood Chowder, **106**
Spicy Mexican-Style Fish
    Stew, **116**
Focaccia Breadsticks, 30
Fresh Mushroom Soup, **174,** 175
Fresh Pea Soup, **179**

G-K

Garbanzo Bean Stew, 152
Garden Chicken Soup, 9
Garlic-Potato Soup, Roasted, 125
Garlic Toasts, 99
Gazpacho To Go, 178
German Potato Soup, 182
Gingered Pumpkin-Pear
    Soup, **164**
Gingersnap Stew, 79
Greek Minestrone, **119, 131**
Green Chile Stew, **62**
Green Onion Biscuits, 30
Gumbo, Classic Chicken-
    Sausage, **40**
Ham
    Brunswick Stew, 41
    Chunky Ham and Potato
        Chowder, 75
    Creamy Ham and Vegetable
        Stew, 78
    Curried Pumpkin Soup, 67
    Curried Split Pea Soup, **72**
    Endive, Ham, and Bean Soup,
        70
    Ham and Vegetable
        Soup, **47, 68**
    New England Ham and Pea
        Soup, 69
Hamburger Soup, 54
Hearty Rice and Sausage
    Soup, 66
Hearty Turkey Soup, 11
Herb and Pepper Lentil Stew, **153**
Herbed Croutons, 99
Hot-and-Sour Tofu Soup, 134
Hot-and-Sour Turkey Soup, 20
Iced Yellow Tomato Soup, 172
Indian Chicken Soup, 12
Italian Bean Soup, 122

Italian Beef Soup, **55**
Italian Chili, 60
Italian Fish and Vegetable
    Soup, 91
Italian Lentil Soup, **128**
Italian Wedding Soup, 52, **53**

L-O

Lamb
    Cassoulet-Style Stew, 84
    Lamb, Lentil, and Onion Soup,
        81
    Lamb Stew with Couscous, **85**
    Lamb Stew with Sweet
        Potatoes, **82,** 83
Leek-Gruyère Cream Soup, **171**
Lemon and Scallop Soup, **97**
Lemon Sour Cream, 165
Lentils
    Beef Stew with Lentils, 64
    Herb and Pepper Lentil
        Stew, **153**
    Italian Lentil Soup, **128**
    Lamb, Lentil, and Onion
        Soup, **81**
    Lamb Stew with Couscous, **85**
    Lentil and Sausage Soup, 73
    Lentil-Spinach Soup, 143
Maryland Crab and Corn
    Chowder, 108
Mashed Sweet Potatoes, 83
Meatball Soup, **50**
Melon
    Farmer's Market Melon Soup,
        186
    Strawberry-Melon Soup, **183**
Mexican Chicken Posole, **21**
Minestrone
    Baby Vegetable
        Minestrone, 181
    Greek Minestrone, **119, 131**
    Minestrone, 161
Moroccan Bouillabaisse, 117
Moroccan Chicken Stew, **42,** 43
Mulligatawny Soup, Easy, **19**
Mushrooms
    Fresh Mushroom
        Soup, **174,** 175
    Mushroom and Tofu Soup, 130
    Pork and Mushroom Soup, 74

New England Ham and Pea
    Soup, 69
Noodles
Asian Chicken Noodle
    Soup, **14,** 15
Carbonnade of Beef and
Vegetables, 65
    Chinese Beef and Noodle
        Soup, 51
North Sea Chowder, 105
Old-Time Beef Stew, 63
Onions
    Caramelized Onion
        Soup, 132, **133**
    Lamb, Lentil, and Onion
        Soup, **81**
Oysters
    Oysters Rockefeller Soup, 166
    Pearl-of-an-Oyster Stew, **115**

P-R

Paella Soup, **95**
Pasta. *See also* Noodles
    A to Z Vegetable
        Soup, 126, **127**
    Chicken Soup with
        Cavatappi, 23
    Chicken Stew with
        Tortellini, 45
    Indian Chicken Soup, 12
    Italian Beef Soup, **55**
    Italian Wedding Soup, 52, **53**
    Pasta and Bean Chicken
        Soup, 28
    Pork and Orzo Soup with
        Spinach, 80
    Shrimp and Coconut
        Soup, 100, **101**
    Squash Soup with Ravioli, **123**
    Tortellini and Vegetable
        Soup, **136**
Peach-Yogurt Soup, Chilled, 184
Peanut Soup, Thai, 124
Pearl-of-an-Oyster Stew, **115**
Pears
    Gingered Pumpkin-Pear
        Soup, **164**
    Sweet Potato and Pear
        Vichyssoise, 170
Peas
    Beefy Vegetable Soup, 49

Curried Split Pea Soup, **72**
Fresh Pea Soup, **179**
New England Ham and Pea
    Soup, 69
Split Pea Soup with Spiced
    Yogurt, 146
Springtime Soup, **121**
Peppers, chile. *See also* Chili
African Chicken Stew, 46
Carrot and Chile Pepper
    Soup, **180**
Chicken Tortilla Soup, 27
Chipotle Chicken Soup, 17
Green Chile Sew, **62**
Ranch Chicken Chowder, 33
Southwestern Bean and
    Chicken Soup, 25
Peppers, sweet
Herb and Pepper Lentil
    Stew, **153**
Red Pepper and Snapper
    Soup, 87, **92**
Red Pepper Soup, 165
Salmon Confetti Chowder, 110
Salmon Pan Chowder, 107
Pork. *See also* Ham, Sausage
Paella Soup, **95**
Pork and Mushroom Soup, 74
Pork and Orzo Soup with
    Spinach, 80
Potatoes. *See also* Sweet
potatoes
Baked Potato Soup, **168**
Bratwurst and Potato Soup, 71
Carolina Catfish Stew, 114
Chunky Ham and Potato
    Chowder, 75
Fennel-Potato Soup, 26
German Potato Soup, 182
Green Chile Stew, **62**
Old-Time Beef Stew, 63
Potato-Beet Soup, **142**
Potato-Curry Soup, 138
Roasted Garlic-Potato
    Soup, 125
Salmon Confetti Chowder, 110
Salsa Verde Beef Stew, **61**
Squash-Potato Chowder, **167**
Pumpkin
Curried Pumpkin Soup, 67

Gingered Pumpkin-Pear Soup,
    164
Quick-to-Fix Turkey and Rice
    Soup, 24
Ranch Chicken Chowder, 33
Ratatouille Stew, Chunky, 156
Red Pepper and Snapper
    Soup, 87, **92**
Red Pepper Soup, 165
Red Seafood Chowder, **106**
Rice. *See also* Wild rice
African Chicken Stew, 46
Asian Turkey and Rice Soup, 22
Catalan Chicken
    Chowder, 7, **34**
Chicken Chili with Rice, 36, **37**
Greek Minestrone, **119**, **131**
Hearty Rice and Sausage
    Soup, 66
Italian Chili, 60
Lentil and Sausage Soup, 73
Paella Soup, **95**
Quick-to-Fix Turkey and Rice
    Soup, 24
Roasted Corn and Crab Soup, 96
Roasted Garlic-Potato Soup, 125
Root Vegetable and Bean
    Soup, 137
Rye Croutons, 26

S

Salmon
Salmon Confetti Chowder, 110
Salmon Pan Chowder, 107
Sherried Salmon Bisque, 103
Salsa Verde Beef Stew, **61**
Sausage
Bratwurst and Potato Soup, 71
Classic Chicken-Sausage
    Gumbo, **40**
Corny Sausage
    Chowder, 76, 77
Gingersnap Stew, 79
Hearty Rice and Sausage
    Soup, 66
Italian Chili, 60
Lentil and Sausage Soup, 73
Tex-Mex Chili, 56
Scallops
Lemon and Scallop Soup, 97

Moroccan Bouillabaisse, 117
Red Seafood Chowder, **106**
Sherried Salmon Bisque, 103
Shrimp
Caribbean Seafood
    Stew, 112, **113**
Creamy Shrimp and Spinach
    Stew, **111**
Effortless Shrimp Chowder,
    109
Moroccan Bouillabaisse, 117
Paella Soup, **95**
Red Seafood Chowder, **106**
Shrimp and Coconut
    Soup, 100, **101**
Shrimp and Greens Soup, **102**
Shrimp-Tortilla Soup, 98
Thai-Style Shrimp Soup, 94
Southwestern Bean and Chicken
    Soup, 25
Spicy Corn Chowder, **104**
Spicy Mexican-Style Fish
    Stew, **116**
Spinach
Chicken Stew with
    Tortellini, 45
Creamy Shrimp and Spinach
    Stew, **111**
Emerald Soup, 141
Greek Minestrone, **119**, **131**
Ham and Vegetable
    Soup, **47**, 68
Lentil-Spinach Soup, 143
Meatball Soup, **50**
Oysters Rockefeller Soup, 166
Pork and Orzo Soup with
    Spinach, 80
Springtime Soup, **121**
Split Pea Soup with Spiced
    Yogurt, 146
Springtime Soup, **121**
Spring Vegetable Soup, **139**
Squash
Bean and Brussels Sprouts
    Stew, **154**, **155**
Chicken Stew with
    Tortellini, 45
Cumin Butternut Squash
    Soup, **177**
Easy Squash Soup, **159**

Garden Chicken Soup, 9
Indian Chicken Soup, 12
Squash-Potato Chowder, **167**
Squash Soup with Ravioli, **123**
Strawberry-Melon Soup, **183**
Sweet potatoes
　Beefy Vegetable Soup, **49**
　Lamb Stew with Sweet
　　Potatoes, **82, 83**
　Mashed Sweet Potatoes, 83
　Sweet Potato and Pear
　　Vichyssoise, 170
　Turkey and Sweet Potato
　　Chowder, 35

T-U

Tex-Mex Chili, 56
Thai Chicken-Coconut Soup, 16
Thai Peanut Soup, 124
Thai-Style Shrimp Soup, 94
Tomatoes
　African Chicken Stew, 46
　Beef and Red Bean
　　Chili, 58, **59**
　Beefy Vegetable Soup, **49**
　Cajun Fish Soup, 89
　Carolina Catfish Stew, 114
　Chicken Tortilla Soup, 27
　Chili with Cornmeal
　　Dumplings, 57
　Fish Soup Provençale, **90**
　Gazpacho To Go, 178
　Greek Minestrone, **119, 131**
　Hamburger Soup, 54
　Iced Yellow Tomato Soup, 172
　Italian Chili, 60
　Minestrone, 161
　Moroccan Chicken
　　Stew, **42,** 43
　North Sea Chowder, 105
　Pasta and Bean Chicken
　　Soup, 28
　Red Seafood Chowder, **106**
　Spicy Mexican-Style Fish
　　Stew, 116
　Tex-Mex Chili, 56
　Two-Tomato Soup, 158
　Vegetable Chili with
　　Cheese, **149**
　White Bean and Cumin
　　Chili, **151**

Tortellini and Vegetable
　Soup, **136**
Tortilla Soup, Chicken, 27
Tortilla Soup, Shrimp-, 98
Turkey
　Asian Turkey and Rice Soup, 22
　Chili Blanco, 38
　Easy Turkey Chowder, 32
　Hearty Turkey Soup, 11
　Hot and Sour Turkey Soup, 20
　Quick-to-Fix Turkey and Rice
　　Soup, 24
　Turkey and Sweet Potato
　　Chowder, 35
　Tutti-Frutti Spiced Fruit
　　Soup, **185**
　Two-Bean Chili, 150
　Two-Tomato Soup, 158

V-Z

Vegetables. *See also specific
vegetable*
　A to Z Vegetable Soup, 126,
　　127
　Baby Vegetable
　　Minestrone, 181
　Beefy Vegetable Soup, **49**
　Carbonnade of Beef and
　　Vegetables, 65
　Chicken and Vegetable Bean
　　Soup, 13
　Chicken Vegetable Ragout, **44**
　Chunky Ratatouille Stew, 156
　Chunky Vegetable-Cod Soup,
　　93
　Creamy Chicken-Vegetable
　　Soup, 18
　Creamy Ham and Vegetable
　　Stew, 78
　Farmer's Vegetable
　　Broth, **157, 173**
　Garden Chicken Soup, **9**
　Greek Minestrone, **119, 131**
　Ham and Vegetable Soup, **47,**
　　68
　Italian Fish and Vegetable
　　Soup, 91
　Minestrone, 161
　Root Vegetable and Bean
　　Soup, 137

Spicy Mexican-Style Fish
　Stew, **116**
Spring Vegetable Soup, **139**
Tortellini and Vegetable
　Soup, **136**
Vegetable Broth, 120
Vegetable Chili with
　Cheese, **149**
Veggie Soup with Curry
　Croutons, **144,** 145
Winter Vegetable Soup, 135
Vichyssoise, Sweet Potato and
　Pear, 170
White Bean and Cumin
　Chili, **151**
White Chili in a Bread Bowl, **39**
Wild rice
　Chicken and Wild Rice
　　Soup, 29
　Wild Rice and Cheese
　　Soup, 129
Winter Vegetable Soup, 135

Tips

Beans, dry 28
Beans, nutritional value of, 25
Bowls, warming and chilling, 78
Broth and stock, freezing, 48
Chicken, cooked, 32
Chile peppers, handling, 12
Slow cooker conversions, 140
Slow cookers, 11, 22
Fish, buying and storing, 88
Garnishes, 99
Ginger, fresh, 51
Herbs, crushing dried, 74
Herbs, substituting dried, 103
Leeks, cleaning, 65
Lentils, types of, 73
Rice vinegar, types of, 134
Salad suggestions, 30
Sandwich suggestions, 30
Shrimp, buying and
　preparing, 117
Sodium in canned broths, 120
Stock, clarifying, 8
Timesavers, 70
Tofu, types of, 130
Tomatoes, peeling and
　seeding, 105

Metric Cooking Hints

By making a few conversions, cooks in Australia, Canada, and the United Kingdom can use the recipes in this book with confidence. The charts on this page provide a guide for converting measurements from the U.S. customary system, which is used throughout this book, to the imperial and metric systems. There also is a conversion table for oven temperatures to accommodate the differences in oven calibrations.

Product Differences: Most of the ingredients called for in the recipes in this book are available in English-speaking countries. However, some are known by different names. Here are some common U.S. ingredients and their possible counterparts:

● Sugar is granulated or castor sugar.
● Powdered sugar is icing sugar.
● All-purpose flour is plain household flour or white flour. When self-rising flour is used in place of all-purpose flour in a recipe that calls for leavening, omit the leavening agent (baking soda or baking powder) and salt.
● Light-color corn syrup is golden syrup.
● Cornstarch is cornflour.
● Baking soda is bicarbonate of soda.
● Vanilla is vanilla essence.
● Green, red, or yellow sweet peppers are capsicums.
● Golden raisins are sultanas.

Volume and Weight: U.S. Americans traditionally use cup measures for liquid and solid ingredients. The chart, above right, shows the approximate imperial and metric equivalents. If you are accustomed to weighing solid ingredients, the following approximate equivalents will help.

● 1 cup butter, castor sugar, or rice = 8 ounces = about 230 grams
● 1 cup flour = 4 ounces = about 115 grams
● 1 cup icing sugar = 5 ounces = about 140 grams

Spoon measures are used for smaller amounts of ingredients. Although the size of the tablespoon varies slightly in different countries, for practical purposes and for recipes in this book, a straight substitution is all that's necessary.

Measurements made using cups or spoons always should be level unless stated otherwise.

Equivalents: U.S. = U.K./Australia

⅛ teaspoon = 1 ml
¼ teaspoon = 1.25 ml
½ teaspoon = 2.5 ml
1 teaspoon = 5 ml
1 tablespoon = 15 ml
1 fluid ounce = 30 ml
¼ cup = 60 ml
⅓ cup = 80 ml
½ cup = 120 ml
⅔ cup = 160 ml
¾ cup = 180 ml
1 cup = 240 ml
2 cups = 475 ml
1 quart = 1 liter
½ inch = 1.25 cm
1 inch = 2.5 cm

Baking Pan Sizes

U.S.	Metric
8×1½-inch round baking pan	20×4-cm cake tin
9×1½-inch round baking pan	23×4-cm cake tin
11×7×1½-inch baking pan	28×18×4-cm baking tin
13×9×2-inch baking pan	32×23×5-cm baking tin
2-quart rectangular baking dish	28×18×4-cm baking tin
15×10×1-inch baking pan	38×25.5×2.5-cm baking tin (Swiss roll tin)
9-inch pie plate	22×4- or 23×4-cm pie plate
7- or 8-inch springform pan	18- or 20-cm springform or loose-bottom cake tin
9×5×3-inch loaf pan	23×13×8-cm or 2-pound narrow loaf tin or pâté tin
1½-quart casserole	1.5-liter casserole
2-quart casserole	2-liter casserole

Oven Temperature Equivalents

Fahrenheit Setting:	Celsius Setting*:	Gas Setting:
300°F	150°C	Gas Mark 2 (very low)
325°F	170°C	Gas Mark 3 (low)
350°F	180°C	Gas Mark 4 (moderate)
375°F	190°C	Gas Mark 5 (moderately hot)
400°F	200°C	Gas Mark 6 (hot)
425°F	220°C	Gas Mark 7 (hot)
450°F	230°C	Gas Mark 8 (very hot)
475°F	240°C	Gas Mark 9 (very hot)
Broil		Grill

*Electric and gas ovens may be calibrated using Celsius. However, for an electric oven, increase the Celsius setting 10 to 20 degrees when cooking above 160°C. For convection or forced-air ovens (gas or electric), lower the temperature setting 10°C when cooking at all heat levels.